SEXUAL FANTASY & THE CHRISTIAN MIND

SEXUAL FANTASY & THE CHRISTIAN MIND

RICA MCPHERSON

SEXUAL FANTASY & THE CHRISTIAN MIND by Rica McPherson©
Published by Rica Mac llc
Lexington, South Carolina 29223

All rights reserved. No part of this publication may be reproduced, distributed, or transmitted in any form or by any means, including photocopying, recording, or other electronic or mechanical methods, without the prior written permission of the publisher, except in the case of brief quotations embodied in critical reviews and specific other noncommercial uses permitted by the United States copyright law.

The information provided in this book is for educational and informational purposes only. It is not intended to replace professional advice or treatment. The author and publisher disclaim any liability arising directly or indirectly from using the information in this book. While the author has exerted her best efforts in preparing this book, she makes no representations or warranties concerning the accuracy or completeness of the contents. It is advisable to consult with a qualified professional when appropriate. The author shall not be held liable for any self-help claims made in this publican. While the author has made every effort to provide accurate information at the time of publication, neither the publisher nor the author assumes any responsibility for errors or for changes that occur after publication.

For permission requests, write to the publisher at the address below.

Rica McPherson
Lexington, South Carolina
ricamac@gmail.com
www.ricamac.com
ISBN: 9798323975532
Published by ricamacllc

Unless otherwise noted, all scripture quotations are taken from the New King James Version®. Copyright © 1982 by Thomas Nelson. Used by permission. All rights reserved.

Copyright licenses by ©2024 Rica McPherson
All rights reserved

Library of Congress Cataloging-in-Publication Data:
Names: Rica McPherson, 1976-author
Title: Sexual Fantasy & The Christian Mind/Rica McPherson
Identifies: LCCN 2024907058|ISBN: 9798323975532
Subjects: Spiritual Religion Christian Life Spiritual growth
LC record available at http://lccn.loc.gov/2024907058

Follow the author online:
    RICA MAC

Author's Note

This book was written to shed light on an area we all face, but only a few are willing to admit publicly. Sexual fantasies are a natural and common occurrence for many people, regardless of their religious beliefs, race, gender, ethnicity, or sexual origin. Some individuals may struggle with feelings of guilt or shame related to sexual fantasies, particularly if they conflict with their beliefs about sexual morality it is important to remember that having sexual desires does not necessarily mean you are engaging in sinful behavior.

However, it is important to consider whether your fantasies align with your personal values and beliefs to ensure that your thoughts and actions are in accordance with those values. Christians may find it helpful to seek guidance and support from their church community, trusted spiritual leaders, or a professional licensed therapist when struggling with issues related to sexual fantasies. Additionally, professional counseling can be beneficial for individuals who are experiencing distress related to their sexual thoughts or behaviors.

Dedication

I dedicate this book to my sons, family, and friends. I am grateful for your unconditional love and support. Thank you all for covering me in your prayers.

Acknowledgment

I would like to thank my mother, sons, siblings, family, and close friends for your continued love and support in my spiritual walk with God. I would also like to thank my spiritual mentor, Pastor Jessie Jackson, (founder of Prayer Walkers of Faith Ministries) for your unwavering dedication, and strong leadership. Your profound guidance, wisdom, time, knowledge, Godly discipline, and love have truly made a lasting impact on my life.

For this is the will of God, your sanctification: that you abstain from **Sexual Immorality**; that each one of you knows How to control his own body in holiness and honor, not in the passion of lust like the Gentiles who do not know God; that no one transgress and wrong his brother in this matter, because the Lord is an avenger in all these things, as we told you beforehand and solemnly warned you. For God has not called us for **impurity**, but **holiness**. Therefore whoever disregards this disregards not man but God, who gives his Holy Spirit to you.[1]

I Thessalonians 4:3-8

CONTENTS

INTRODUCTION UNCHARTED TERRITORIES

    Uncharted Territories............................1

    The Landscape of Desire...................3

CHAPTER 1 UNDERSTANDING SEXUAL FANTASY

    Understanding Sexual Fantasy....................7

    What Is Sexual Fantasy...............................8

    Is It Wrong to Fantasize.............................11

    Samson's Sexual Sin..................................16

    Avoiding Sexual Sin...................................20

    Signs of Sexual Fantasies...........................25

CHAPTER 2 THE PURPOSE OF SEXUAL FANTASIES (THE EROTIC MIND)

    The Purpose of Sexual Fantasies.....................29

    Cultural Influences.......................................30

    The Christian Mind and Sexuality 31

    The Effects of an erotic mind 33

    The sexual sin of King Herod.......................34

    Fantasy and the mind 35

    Sexual fantasies & the single Christian............37

    Sexual fantasies & the married Christian.........38

    The Dangers of Unrestrained Fantasies..........39

    The wrong thoughts.....................................39

Why is this happening?...........................40
Sexual Fantasies & the Mind of a Christian....41
The sensitive topic of sexual fantasies..........43

CHAPTER 3 CHILDHOOD & SEXUALLY

Childhood and sexuality……………………......47
How were you introduced to sex?….................48
How did you lose your virginity?…................52
The Fatherless Child………………………......54
Middle school days……………………………57
The forbidden fruit……………………………58
The rape that left you silent ………………….59
Dealing with sexual fetish ……………………60
Getting the monkey off your back…………….61
The adult view………………………………...62
The root of it all …....………………….....…..64
The sexual sin of King David……………........65

CHAPTER 4 MASTURBATION: THE POWER OF A TOUCH

The power of a touch……………………….....69
Spirit Spouse…………………………………..75
Planting a seed………………………………...79
Mind Control Spirits…………………………..81
Laying on of hands…………………………....82
Weird warfare…………………………………83
Covering your gates……………………….….84
The eyes……………………………………....86

ii

The ear……………………………………………..89
The mouth…………………………………...............90
The nose……………………………………………91
The heart……………………………………………92
The hands……………………………………………92
The feet…………………………………………….93
Breaking free………………………………………95
A byproduct of sexual fantasy…………………....96
Gaining control over lust……………………….98
Christianity & sexual purity………………….....100
A Distorted View of Sexuality………………103
A Hindrance to your spiritual growth………......103

CHAPTER 5   GODLY DATING

Godly dating…………………………………105
How can I find someone?………………………107
Why am I still single?……………………………115
Single & saved………………………..………….117
Embracing singleness in ministry………………118
Breaking the Stigma…………………………….119
Your spiritual well-being……………………….120
Long courtship…………..………………………121
The right one……...………………………………124
Out with the old in with the new…..………….130
A better option……………..….,………………..131
They belong to the streets ………………………132
Sex before marriage………………………………133

Singleness & the church 136
Hold on do not lose hope........................... 137

CHAPTER 6 SEXUAL FANTASIES & YOUR MARRIAGE

Sexual fantasies & your marriage....…............139
Exchange of vows..…......…......................140
What is a vow?….....…..............................141
Marriage is a ministry………......................142
Wedded Bliss!...146
Dyadic Fantasies……..................................149
Sexual Satisfaction…...................................150
Sexual Misconduct in a Marriage..................153
Craving the touch of another….....................154
Divorcing your spirit spouse..…....................157
Sex after divorce………...............................161

CHAPTER 7 OVERCOMING THE GUILT & SHAME

Eliminating negative self-talk…....................165
Understanding guilt & shame…....................167
Seeking professional guidance…..................168
Separating fantasy from reality….................170
Religion & societal expectations…...............171
Cultivating a positive sexual narrative...........172
Letting go of the pain…...............................174
Overcoming sexual fantasies…....................177
A Faith-Based Approach……......................178
Self-Compassion….....…............................180

Finding your safe space…………………………...183

PRAYER

Repentance ……………………………………....190

Overcoming childhood trauma…………………..191

Generational Curse……………………………….192

The singles……………………………………….193

The married ……………………………………...194

Masturbation & sexual perversion……,…………196

CHAPTER 8   THE AUTHOR'S EXPERIENCE

Where it all began………………………………...197

Escaping abuse……………………………………199

Keep it moving…………………………………….200

Make it stop……………………………………….201

Afraid of the terror……………………………….203

Tell no one………………………………………..205

Time is up………………………………………...207

Pack your stuff & get out.…..……………………209

I Stopped going to church….……………………..210

The man of my dreams …………………………..210

I Fell……………………………………………...212

The Betrayal……………………………………...214

NOTES:

INTRODUCTION
UNCHARTED TERRITORIES

"If we confess our sins, he is faithful and just and will forgive us our sins and purify us from all unrighteousness."

-I John 1:9

In a world often filled with hushed whispers and uneasy glances, it is time to embark on a journey that explores the intricate relationship between sexuality, desire, and faith. In this book, "**Sexual Fantasy and the Christian Mind**." We set out to address a topic that has long been considered taboo within the context of Christianity. As a Christian believer, living with sexual fantasies can be a heavy burden on your conscience. This is a distinct experience from that of someone who is an unbeliever. Shame and silence often plague Christians, leaving them feeling as if they have no safe space to express the thoughts residing in their minds.

Despite the comfort and hope these fantasies offer, along with a temporary escape from the monotony of life, internal conflicts and guilt can be overwhelming. Sexual fantasies may appear harmless since they only exist in your mind, and you are not acting on them. Consequently, you may question who they are hurting. They are privately hidden beneath the surface and only appear when you need them, such as late at night when you are having problems falling asleep or when your stress level gets high, and you need an escape.

Sexual Fantasy & The Christian Mind

Sexual fantasies, though intensely personal and multifaceted, are an undeniable aspect of the human experience. They possess the power to stir emotions, ignite passion, and sometimes leave you with questions of morality and spirituality. However, the intersection of these desires and Christian beliefs can lead to complex inner discourse, creating emotional imbalances in the believer's life. With the utmost respect for the Christian faith and its teachings, this book aims to provide a safe space for open conversation and introspection. It seeks to navigate the uncharted territories of sexual fantasy, encouraging readers to confront their desires while remaining true to their Christian values.

Throughout these pages, we will take a deeper look at the inner workings of your mind behind sexual fantasies that intertwine psychology, theology, and personal narratives. We will explore the origins of your thoughts, dissect common misconceptions, and confront the dichotomy between the sacred and the erotic. Through it all, we strive to foster a deeper understanding of how your faith can form and shape your attitude toward sexuality. This book does not aim to prescribe a singular set of rules or to offer definitive answers. Instead, it invites you to thoroughly examine your desires and beliefs, empowering you to enter a personal exploration that aligns with your Christian faith.

A Christian's psyche is woven in faith. Ephesians 2:8-9 reads *"For by grace you have been saved through faith. And this is not your own doing; it is the gift of God, not a result of works, so that no one may boast."*[1]

Knowing this the dialogue becomes layered with theological considerations, moral reflections, and the ongoing pursuit of spiritual growth. Navigating **"Sexual Fantasy and the Christian Mind"** will take you into a contemplative exploration that transcends the complex path where faith connects with the rich landscape of human desire.

Introduction: Uncharted Territories

Sexuality and spirituality are often seen as separate realms, one representing good and the other representing evil, creating a delicate dance within the Christian framework of desire and belief. The observation of sexual fantasies within this context is laden with questions, contradictions, and a yearning for understanding. As we begin this exploration in search of answers, it is crucial to approach the subject with openness, sensitivity, and a commitment to fostering communication that goes beyond taboos and embraces the complexity of the human experience.

This sets the stage for a reflective look at some of the past mistakes you have made concerning sexual misconduct in the Christian faith. What made you do it? And how can you stop it from happening again? By acknowledging the challenges, celebrating the diversity of perspectives, and paving the way for a more compassionate understanding of the convergence between sexual fantasies and the Christian mind. This information will help you gain control over your sexual urges through the blood of the lamb.

THE LANDSCAPE OF DESIRE

Sexual impulse is an integral part of the human experience. It is a force that propels us forward, influencing our thoughts, actions, and relationships within Christianity. Where themes of love, intimacy, and purity are central, sexual needs take on a unique significance. Experiencing sexual fantasies often exists in the interplay of our physical, emotional, and spiritual dimensions.

It is a realm where the boundaries between the holy and the profane may blur, prompting individuals to navigate the tension between their innate sexual cravings and the moral teachings of their faith. Understanding the thirst within the Christian mind requires a spiritual approach from the biblical narratives that encourage us not to lust after the beauty of human creation to the complex reflections of today's worldly expression of sexual freedom with the person of your choice.

Sexual Fantasy & The Christian Mind

This excursion invites you to consider how the modern-day church and its traditional practices have struggled with this intricate aspect of human sexuality.

"Behold, I was sharpen in iniquity; And in sin did my mother conceive me" Psalm 51:1. [1]

The imbalance of good and evil began with Adam and Eve's disobedience in the garden. Their lack of self-control caused mankind to be born with a propensity toward committing evil. As a child, you naturally gravitated towards lying and engaging in sinful behavior without needing instructions, it happened automatically. When you emerged from your mother's womb, it was not with Godly virtues but rather with a mind filled with evil instinct taking the lead. Your upbringing was influenced by your inherent sinful nature and the prevailing influence of your authentic self, ultimately molding you into the person you became. This is why you were exposed to sexual perversion at a young age.

The biblical revelations provided in this book will leave you with a clear understanding of the complexities of sex between a man and a woman in the Christian context. How can you reconcile your humanity with the teachings of your faith? What Biblical frameworks are required for understanding the role of passion in the life of a Christian? Religious leaders often caution against blaming the devil for the struggles with sexual sin without being transparent, which leads to a perplexing question. If it is not the powers of darkness at work then why do esteemed leaders succumb to ungodly sexual acts themselves?

The nature of sin has more contemporary divine perspectives emphasizing the goodness of creation, which contributes to our understanding of God's intention. These perspectives help us recognize the desire when dealing with sexual fantasies and moral views.

Introduction: Uncharted Territories

Theological reflections help us discern the ethical aspects of our fantasies, giving us a basis for managing sexual desire from a Christian perspective. This point of view contributes to our comprehension of desire and offers guidance in navigating the moral dimensions of our fantasies through theological reflections which lead us to discern these doctrinal heights. It offers a foundation upon which we can navigate sexual desire within the Christian mind. The information in this book may challenge established norms and push the boundaries of the comfort you are used to.

Yet, it is within this tension that growth, healing, and a more nuanced understanding can be found. Therefore, I invite you to approach these pages with an open mind, a compassionate heart, and a willingness to work through the complexities that lie ahead. May **"Sexual Fantasy and the Christian Mind"** serve as a guiding light for the person seeking reconciliation between their deepest desires and their Christian identity. In the realm of human experiences, few subjects evoke as much fascination, curiosity, and, at times, discomfort as sexual fantasies.

CHAPTER ONE
UNDERSTANDING SEXUAL FANTASY

"The desire to love is to give.
The desire of lust is to take."
-**Chery & Chery** [2]

A fantasy is a creation of the imagination, often involving acts or events that are impossible or unlikely to occur under normal circumstances.[3] When it comes to sexual fantasies, however, that is not the case. These fantasies can become a reality given enough time and the right opportunity. Sexual fantasy revolves around imagining sexual acts or events. However, depending on the content and the individuals involved, sexual fantasy can be morally or ethically inappropriate. Therefore, it is essential to note that any fantasy scenario that goes against moral, ethical, or spiritual values is regarded as sinful. Imagination is a precious gift bestowed upon you by God, and fantasizing is an integral part of the human psyche.

We frequently engage in fantasizing without knowing. Fantasies can range from envisioning favorable circumstances, like clear traffic on the way to work, to enjoying a peaceful vacation on the beach. These fantasies often emerge from your reality and serve as attempts to create an idealized version of existence rather than accepting the realities of life. Some individuals become so engrossed in fantasy that they disconnect from reality and genuine relationships.

Sexual Fantasy & The Christian Mind

Since the invention of the internet, sexting, virtual porn hubs, and social media have all provided various avenues for people to create virtual personas. Allowing them to experience life vicariously through these characters within these cybernetic realms. Sexual fantasies often play a significant role, enabling individuals to simulate sexual acts without physically being present. However, it is essential to recognize that while engaging in indirect sexual fantasies. You must remain conscious that your actions do not reflect God's will for your life, nor do they align with your Christian values and beliefs.

WHAT IS SEXUAL FANTASY?

"Sexual fantasy is an imagined sexual scene that intensifies emotional and physical excitement by helping people play out their most intense sexual desires, fears, or memories. Fantasies may remain as hidden impulses in the unconscious or desire that are fully conscious and recognized."[3] Fantasizing connects to your imaginative capabilities, constituting an integral aspect of the daydreaming process. This "phenomenon occurs within the brain's temporal lobe region, explicitly involving the hippocampus. The hippocampus assumes a pivotal function in your capacity to envision and engage in daydreaming"[4] activities.

Single Christians are advised to refrain from engaging in any sexual activities until they are married. This expectation was more attainable in the past due to the prevailing mindset shared by men, women, parents, the community, and even church leaders. Society nurtured and guided young people towards marriage, which resulted in strong and enduring unions between husbands and wives. However, in this era, many individuals have distanced themselves from the church and are navigating the world without spiritual guidance. They believe in a higher power but not necessarily in God.

Chapter One: Understanding Sexual Fantasy

This new-age reality has resulted in decreased accountability and solidarity within communities, leaving many to fend for themselves. The idea of getting married is no longer viewed as a desirable topic of conversation for both men and women, especially among the younger generation. Young adults are being encouraged to forge their own path based on their intellectual beliefs. It is the "Boss Chic, and I am a KING era." Married individuals find themselves envying those who are single as they battle the fear of missing out on life experiences due to the added responsibility of managing a family. This shift in mindset has brought us to a point where many prioritize sexual gratification over living holy.

While this may not pose a problem for those who do not hold Christian values, it presents an obstacle for individuals committed to upholding biblical principles. Living as a single Christian in modern times presents unique challenges when practicing abstinence. Asking a sixteen-year-old to abstain from sex may be more attainable than asking the same request of an adult who has already engaged in sexual activities. This request becomes difficult because the teenager is at a disadvantage, having never had sex. They have no soul-ties or entanglements to overcome (this only holds true for teens who are still virgins).

Although they may struggle with sexual fantasies, their lack of experience and fear of going against their parents' warnings and God's teachings often prevent them from acting on these desires. On the other hand, adults who have had multiple sexual partners and experiences face a greater temptation. Society often frames these desires as natural needs that must be met. This makes them more challenging to overcome while striving to uphold Christian values. The prevailing mindset surrounding the sustainability of Christian abstinence from sexual pleasure for an extended period creates a false narrative.

Sexual Fantasy & The Christian Mind

Most single Christians often feel neglected by their church, and very few churches prioritize regular fellowship for singles. The topic of sex and Christianity remains taboo and is rarely discussed publicly in church settings. The singles' ministry is either put on the back burner or on life support in many churches. Anyone courageous enough to bring up the topic of sex in a religious setting is swiftly rebuked and silenced. When someone within the church exhibits what others deem to be ungodly behavior, they are subjected to an intense barrage of scriptures, dragged to the altar, and urged to renounce their perceived acts of the flesh.

Consequently, more and more young people are drifting away from the faith, adopting a Christian chameleon approach, conforming to their environment rather than adhering to God's word. The only advice church leaders seem to offer regarding sex is to "abstain." While living a sexless life as a Christian may seem manageable in the short term, it is certainly not sustainable for longer periods. How does a Christian who has been single for five, ten, fifteen, or even twenty years cope with the urges of feeling horny & holy? These questions remain unanswered, and the church lacks guidance and support in addressing the unique struggles faced by long-term singleness.

This neglect leaves individuals struggling with their faith. As the years go by, the hope of finding a spouse or meeting the right person diminishes, and a sense of isolation, loneliness, rejection, and aloneness takes hold. This leaves a significant number of single Christians yearning for an escape. Weary of waiting, they create an alternate universe in their minds, a perfect world where they can seek relief from the wait. Unfortunately, this opens demonic portals that leads to weird spiritual warfare and the kingdom of sexual perversion.

Chapter One: Understanding Sexual Fantasy

IS IT WRONG TO FANTASIZE?

Fantasy, in its essence, is not intrinsically harmful. It is a skill we acquire in childhood, often nurtured by the enchanting fairy tales that were read to us during Storytime or before bedtime. However, sexual fantasies can be considered the darker side of imagination. It has the potential to instigate inner conflicts within the Christian mind, aiming to lure individuals into a perplexing expedition down the rabbit hole. If left unchecked, you may find yourself in a bewildering state like Alice in Wonderland, trying to figure out how you got there. Fantasizing is a natural human tendency, and nothing is inherently wrong with it.

However, it is essential to recognize that sexual fantasies can sow corruptible seeds in your mind. In I Peter 1:23, God encourages us to be born again not of corruptible seed but of incorruptible seed by the word of God[1]. As you continue to indulge in the thought process of creating this idealized, problem-free world, the seed begins to sprout into full-blown sexual fantasies. The prolonged indulgence in such thoughts can lead to the development of elaborate scenarios in your mind. Proverbs 23:7 reads, *"For as a man thinketh in his heart so is he."*[1] The critical emphasis lies in the word "*think*."

Our thoughts originate in our minds, and when we fantasize, these thoughts transform into desires that take root in our hearts. It is crucial to recognize that ungodly desires, nurtured over time, can dull our spiritual swords and gifts. Consequently, this weakening can create vulnerabilities in your mind for the enemy to gain influence over you and make a mess of your life. Thus, you should be mindful of your thought life and strive to align your desires with God's will to guard against spiritual vulnerability. *"A little leaven leaveneth the whole lump"* (Galatians 5:9).[1]

Sexual Fantasy & The Christian Mind

You may argue as to whether you are doing anything wrong. The Bible emphasizes the importance of your pure thoughts and clarifies that even our fantasies should be brought under submission to God's will. Jesus spoke about the connection between our hearts and our speech, stating that what we say reflects what is in our hearts and can defile us. He explained that evil thoughts, such as murder, adultery, sexual immorality, theft, false testimony, and slander, originate from the heart (Matt. 15.19).[1] Additionally, Jesus pointed out that looking at someone with lustful intent is equivalent to committing adultery in the heart (Matt. 5.28).[1]

If sexual fantasy involves actions or words contrary to God's will, it becomes a sin. If a married individual fantasizes about their spouse, it is not thought of as sinful. The marital relationship is regarded as honorable, and the married bed is seen as pure and undefiled, as mentioned in (Heb. 13.4).[1] However, if these thoughts involve entertaining the idea of engaging in sexual acts with someone other than their spouse, it ventures into the territory of lust, which is acknowledged as sinful. It is essential for you to align your thoughts with God's standards, avoiding impure and inappropriate desires by concentrating on what is honorable and in accordance with God's will for your life.

Human sexuality is a complex and diverse aspect of life, encompassing many thoughts, desires, and behaviors. Within this spectrum, sexual fantasies hold a significant place. It contains realistic and unrealistic scenarios, reflecting an individual's unique preferences and imagination. Sexual fantasies often play a crucial role in generating and enhancing sexual arousal serving as an outlet for physical, emotional, and psychological needs. It also acts as a coping mechanism temporarily relieving everyday stressors, worries, and anxieties. Additionally, sexual fantasies can contribute to exploring one's sexual identity and establishing a stronger sense of self.

Chapter One: Understanding Sexual Fantasy

It is essential to understand that sexual fantasies are a natural and expected part of human sexuality. They serve various purposes: arousal, emotional fulfillment, exploration, and stress relief. Recognizing that these fantasies exist within the realm of imagination and do not necessarily reflect an individual's real-life desires or actions is crucial. They should be understood and approached with a balanced perspective, acknowledging their role in human sexuality while maintaining a clear distinction between fantasy and reality. Being a single Christian in today's world is undeniably challenging.

Christians are constantly bombarded with sexual content through various outlets such as movies, television shows, social media, work environments, magazines, books, and virtually all aspects of life. The Christian perspective has undergone significant changes over the years. We have shifted from a generation of Christians who embraced the natural progression of aging to believers who now dictate how we age. The prevalent notion that "you have needs and God understands" has subtly influenced our thinking and choices. In the past, Christians would leave the club late at night before attending church the following morning.

Now, they roll out of bed with their recent hook-up on Sunday morning. It begs the question: How did we reach this point where sexual sin has become so normalized? Sin can only exist in the absence of God. When we grow weary in our walk with God, our minds seek alternative paths to continue our faith. Sometimes, this leaves us feeling as if God has turned His back on us. This can lead to a desperate search for an escape from our struggles. Navigating the complexities of living a faithful Christian life as a single person in today's society is undoubtedly difficult.

Sexual Fantasy & The Christian Mind

It requires steadfast commitment, a firm foundation in our faith, constant reliance on God's guidance, and strength to resist the allure of what is considered the sexual norms that surround us. There is a lack of knowledge on navigating the terrain of sexuality as a modern-day Christian.

Hosea 4:6 reads, *"My people are destroyed from lack of knowledge. Because you have rejected knowledge, I also reject you as my priests. Because you have ignored the law of your God, I also will ignore your children."*[1]

This verse indicates that God will reject us when we reject him. However, sometimes it feels like God is not with us, although we accepted him. Feeling this way can be attributed to you not knowing the ways of God. In today's church, singleness is treated as a crime, sickness, or disease. Single Christians are often ridiculed and made to feel ashamed for even desiring to marry. Frequently, they are faced with the monotony of life. The convolutedness of their life leaves them in a continued state of transition.

They end their teen years, enter adulthood, and then begin executing life's milestones like getting married, having children, landing their dream job, and creating their version of happily ever after, but what happens when life throws them a curve ball? What happens when they find themselves divorced because the marriage did not go according to plan? How do they navigate life? Or maybe they have never been married, they gave their life to Christ at a young age, and now they are in their forties, and no one has shown interest in them as a spouse or even asked for their hand in marriage. What is the protocol for someone who has lived in abstinence for years?

Chapter One: Understanding Sexual Fantasy

Asking a person to exercise self-discipline and self-control in abstinence for decades is an unrealistic goal to ask of anyone. Why are church leaders not doing more to foster an environment of marriages in churches? Families are the cornerstone of the community, so why is this not being encouraged? We know the Bible tells us *"With God, all things are possible"* (Matt. 19.26).[1] However sexual fantasies developed in the minds of believers give them a safe space to create an alternative reality to engage in sexual acts without feeling guilty.

The problem with engaging in these fantasies is the direct access it gives the world of darkness into your life; Isaiah 5:18 reads, *"Woe unto them that draw iniquity with cords of vanity, and sin as it were with a cart rope."*[1] This is the result of sexual fantasies in the mind of the Christian believer. It is designed to move you out of right standing with God. When you allow these thoughts to occupy your mind over time, the feeling of these thoughts manifests in your body, which leads to masturbation. We will discuss this more in-depth in chapter four. Indulging in sexual fantasies before falling asleep will manifest in your natural body the following morning.

A woman will discover discharge in her underwear and a male may wake up with an erection and semen on his clothing. The imagery of these visual acts in your mind opened a portal for demonic spirits to come in and have sex with you in your sleep. This leaves your body feeling as if you experienced the actual act, which in turn causes you to climax, leading to a sexual release. These demonic spirits, also known as **Incubus** (the demon that has sex with women in their sleep) and **Succubus** (the demon that has sex with men in their sleep)[5], are there to create a sexual stronghold in your life that will expose you to the kingdom of sexual perversion.

These spirits are there to take over your life and ultimately destroy your relationship with God. Once the portal is open, these demonic forces have the legal right to lay hold on your children and corrupt your bloodline by creating generational curses. Each time you engage in sexual acts with these spirits, you are entering into a dark covenant that leads to a spiritual marriage, creating spirit wives and husbands. This gives them the right to upset your finances and inflict your body with sickness. Engaging in the realm of sexual misconduct is intended to diminish your lifespan and lead to your downfall.

The further you explore these thoughts and indulge in such behaviors, the more you will discover yourself descending into a downward spiral, losing control along the way. The end goal of these demonic spirits is to blind your spiritual eyes and abort your destiny in God. Going down this path may lead to an untimely death. John 10:10 reads, *"The thief comes only to steal and kill and destroy I have come that they may have life and have it more abundantly."*[1]

The Bible reads, *"But we are tempted when we are drawn away and trapped by our evil desires. Then our evil desires conceive and give birth to sin, and sin, when it is full-grown, gives birth to death. Do not be deceived, my dear friends"* (Jas. 1.14-16).[1] All forms of sin start as a seed, but once it blossoms, it produces the fruit of death, whether spiritual or natural.

SAMSON'S SEXUAL SIN (JUDGES. 16:18-22)[1]

God gave Samson clear directives on whom he should associate with, considering his extraordinary powers. Samson was permitted to marry a woman from Timnah as part of a divine strategy to fulfill his destiny of defeating the Philistines and liberating his people. Although he managed to evade the traps set by his first wife, he encountered a formidable adversary in Delilah.

Chapter One: Understanding Sexual Fantasy

His involvement in sexual misconduct with a prostitute set the stage for Delilah to enter his life. She was bribed by the Philistine army to discover the source of his strength so they could use it to their advantage against him. Witnessing the tragic death by fire that was carried out on Samson's first wife and her father by the Philistine army. Delilah accepted the task, she understood the assignment and knew that failure was not an option. Samson may have been trained in the art of war, but Delilah was a professional seductress who operated under the demonic spirit of the **black widow spider** (Job 8:14-15, Isaiah 59:5).[6]

This demon represents toxic love. Being drawn to this spirit starts with an intense attraction that feels erotic. Your attraction to the person possessed with this spirit is alluring because they are leading you to their evil layer to disarm you of your spiritual gifts, which is where your power in God lies. Their job is to strip you of your spiritual strength by getting you to lower your defenses and have sex with them so they can extract information. Delilah was also connected to the Marine Kingdom.

Judges 16:23 reads, *"Now the rulers of the Philistines assembled to offer a great sacrifice to Dagon, their god, and to celebrate, saying, "Our god has delivered Samson, our enemy, into our hands."*[1]

Dagon is known as the fish god, he is part man, part fish. Delilah was paid 1100 pieces of silver to betray Samson. Anyone who accepts money or gifts from this kingdom agrees with their practices, which means she also would have operated under the spell of a marine spirit.

Sexual Fantasy & The Christian Mind

Delilah never reciprocated Samson's love. This is because she was on assignment and had to maintain focus, catching feelings was not a part of the plan and she knew it. The more Samson had sex with Delilah, the weaker he became. Having sex with yourself or an agent of darkness weakens your defenses and opens you up for demonic enslavement. Samson was not in a relationship with Delilah; he was in a situationship like many of you are today. An agent of darkness will always ask you to trust them, knowing they are not worthy of your trust.

Isaiah 59:19 reads, *"Fear the name of the LORD from the west and His glory from the rising of the sun; When the enemy comes in like a flood, The Spirit of the LORD will lift up a standard against him."*[1]

The enemy can only come in to destroy you when you lower your standards, which is God's defense in your life. It was not the will of God for Samson to be with Delilah. She belonged to the streets, and he should have left her there, but because she was sexy and seductive, he took her to the sheets and in the end, he died prematurely because of his actions. Delilah caused Samson to break his Nazirite vow with God. The enemy is doing the same thing to many of you today, but remember Ecclesiastes 5:4-6 reads, *"When you make a vow to God, do not delay in fulfilling it. He has no pleasure in fools; fulfill your vow. It is better not to vow than to make a vow and not fulfill it. Do not let your mouth lead you into sin."*[1]

Employing her sexual allure, she lured the man of God into the intricacies of her trap, exploiting his penchant for danger. In his negligence, Samson treated Delilah's inquiries about the origin of his strength lightly. Blinded by his sexual desire for her and a growing appetite for more, each encounter with Delilah bore a hole in Samson's spiritual armor.

Chapter One: Understanding Sexual Fantasy

This mirrors the ongoing struggle faced by Christians who succumb to sexual fantasies. In verses 18-22, Samson eventually disclosed the truth about his strength to Delilah. However, verse 20 poignantly notes, *"but he didn't realize the LORD had left him." Samsom lost the favor of God in his life,"*[1] This reflects the plight of modern-day Christians entangled in sexual immorality. Often, they fail to recognize God's favor and glory have departed from their life, leaving them in a state of desolation and confusion. Delilah realized Samson finally told her the truth, so she sent for the Philistine rulers.

"Come back one more time," she said, "for he has finally told me his secret."[1] *So, the Philistine rulers returned with the money in their hands. "Delilah lulled Samson to sleep with his head in her lap, and then she called in a man to shave off the seven locks of his hair. She began to bring him down,*[a] *and his strength left him."*[1]

The devil sends agents of darkness into your life to tear you down and sexual fantasy is the door he uses for them to enter in. Verse 22 reads, *"But before long, his hair began to grow back."*[1] Sexual sin blinds your natural and spiritual eyes. It leaves you in a posture of weird spiritual warfare, this level of entanglement makes it hard for you to see yourself the way God sees you. Samson's hair began to grow back, but it did not change the fact that he was being held captive by his enemy and was bound and gagged. This is what sin does, it entraps you by taking away your free will to serve God.

2 Timothy 2:26 reads, *"Then they will come to their senses and escape from the devil's trap. For they have been held captive by him to do whatever he wants."*[1]

Sexual Fantasy & The Christian Mind

Engaging in sexual sin gives the enemy the right to enslave you and exercise total ownership over your life. Sex with Delilah dulled Samson's senses. He lost all rational reasoning. She had three failed attempts on his life before succeeding. His deductive reasoning should have told him after the first attempt to stay away from her because she should not be trusted. So, what kept him running back to the arms of Lady Danger? It is the same thing that keeps many of you returning to yours. It is a soul-tie entanglement rooted in strong divination laced with occultic practices.

Once he met her, God was out, and Delilah was in. As he allowed his spiritual state to become diminished it caused him to operate in doubt, which led him to reveal his secret to the enemy. The way she did that thing, that she did, the way she did it! Had him wide open to the point where it caused him to doubt what the angel of God told his parents before he was born. He believed he would still be strong even if his hair were cut. This is what sex does to a Christian once it pulls them outside the will of God. You begin sharing secrets God told you about your destiny with the devil.

AVOIDING SEXUAL SIN

The Holy Spirit will not dwell in an unclean temple. Continuing down a path of sexual sin, issues an automatic eviction notice to the Holy Spirit. The enemy's goal is to create a vacancy in you by getting God out so he can move in. Once his mission is accomplished he takes over your mind, body, and soul. Leaving you Walking blindly in the spirit realm which can lead to spiritual miscarriages and aborted destiny.

Chapter One: Understanding Sexual Fantasy

1 Corinthians 6:12-20 reads, *"I am allowed to do anything"—but not everything is good for you. And even though "I am allowed to do anything," I must not become a slave to anything. You say, "Food was made for the stomach, and the stomach for food. (This is true, though someday God will do away with both of them.) But you can't say that our bodies were made for sexual immorality. They were made for the Lord, and the Lord cares about our bodies. And God will raise us from the dead by his power, just as he raised our Lord from the dead.*[1]

Don't you realize that your bodies are actually parts of Christ? Should a man take his body, which is part of Christ, and join it to a prostitute? Never! And don't you realize that if a man joins himself to a prostitute, he becomes one body with her? For the Scriptures say, "The two are united into one." But the person who is joined to the Lord is one spirit with him. Run from sexual sin! No other sin so clearly affects the body as this one does. Sexual immorality is a sin against your own body. Don't you realize that your body is the temple of the Holy Spirit, who lives in you and was given to you by God? You do not belong to yourself, for God bought you with a high price. So, you must honor God with your body."[1]

A Christian who becomes entangled in impure thoughts will engage in spiritual warfare of the mind; I Peter 1:13 reads, *"Therefore, prepare your minds for action, keep sober in spirit, and fix your hope entirely on the grace to be brought to you at the revelation of Jesus Christ."*[1] Entertaining sexual fantasies renders you useless in God. You are not thinking with a clear and sober mind because you are drunk with lust and unable to receive divine revelation from God, engaging in these thoughts block your spiritual transmitters and dulls your sharpness in the spirit realm.

Sexual Fantasy & The Christian Mind

"For the weapons of our warfare are not carnal, but mighty through God to the pulling down of strong holds; Casting down imaginations, and every high thing that exalted itself against the knowledge of God and bringing into captivity every thought to the obedience of Christ; And having in a readiness to revenge all disobedience when your obedience is fulfilled" (2 Cor. 10.3-6).[1]

If you persist in indulging in these fantasies without casting down vain imaginations, dismantling high places, and tearing down strongholds, the devil gains legal rights to establish strongholds in your life. As a born-again Christian, you possess the power to resist the devil, and as per James 4:7, *he will "flee from you."*[1] Flee implies running away from a place or situation of danger.[7] This definition indicates that when you resist the devil, you hold the upper hand, and he rapidly retreats because you rejected his advances. A Christian with the strength to resist the devil poses a significant threat to his kingdom.

This is the reason he sends sexual thoughts to your mind in the form of fantasies; these thoughts weaken your deficiencies. Once he takes control of your mind with these explicit thoughts. Your spiritual defenses are compromised, and even if you see him coming. The guilt and shame from entertaining these fantasies make it difficult for you to fight. God wants to use your spiritual gifts for his glory and the devil wants to use them to defile you, by increasing your fleshly desire. He starts with harmless fantasies, then shift you to sexual fantasies, then he promotes you to porn. Next, he moves you to self-pleasure (also known as masturbation).

Then, after a while, you begin craving the touch of a person. You want to be kissed, caressed, massaged, aroused and rubbed down. By this point, you will find yourself wanting a warm body next to you to act out all your sexual exploits.

Chapter One: Understanding Sexual Fantasy

Once you venture out of God, to find a partner who appeases your flesh, it does not take long for you to discover you found the freak of the week. This is a person who is trisexual and they are willing to engage in all forms of sexual sin. Their agenda is to become a drug in your system and get you addicted to their touch. Just like Delilah, this is an agent of darkness on assignment. Who is working in conjunction with hell to turn you out. Their goal is to take you past soul ties into full-on entanglement. The devil has anointed them to decode your spirituality with every touch.

They are designed to meet all your sexual needs. The enemy wants to make a mockery of you in the sight of God by taking you deeper into sexual sin; he plans to get you to a place of having a reprobate mind. He wants to turn you out by being your spiritual pimp. Each time you commit sexual sin, then ask for forgiveness and repeat the behavior, it separates you from God. This advances you closer to having a reprobate mind. Which means you become morally depraved, unprincipled, and evil. Rejected by God and beyond hope of salvation. [8] Being in a state of reprobate will leave you feeling indifferent. You are not in the body or out of the body, you are just existing by occupying time and space on Earth.

Your mind is set on autopilot, and you are just going through the motions. You are still able to smile and quote scriptures. But somewhere in your mind, you feel lost, dazed, and confused because your mind constantly thinks about the sins you are committing. You sometimes wonder if what you are doing is wrong because, in your heart, you believe that if it were, God would have exposed you to your spiritual leaders. Here is the truth: you are not getting away with it; God is sitting back, watching you play a game of Russian roulette with your salvation, hoping you will come to your senses before it is too late.

Sexual Fantasy & The Christian Mind

If you should die right now before having a chance to repent. Where would you spend eternity? With each passing day, you become a carbon copy of your former self, hating the person looking back at you in the mirror. You desperately want to stop but have no idea how to stop! You take intermittent breaks, which create the illusion of freedom, only for you to find yourself awakening a few days later with a craving for a sexual touch. In this backslidden state, the crucial step is to be ready to repent and reconcile with God, returning to a state of righteousness. If the urges overpower your will to repent, earnestly ask God to turn your heart back to Him and guide you toward a place of readiness for restoration by the leading of the Holy Spirit.

Make a firm decision today to regain control of your life. Choose to do what is right both in private and in public. God, knows you desire you to be a vessel of honor, not dishonor (2 Tim. 2.20-23).[1] Despite engaging in spiritual warfare with the devil's tools, remember that God still delivers. Today, He aims to liberate you from all forms of sexual fantasies and perversion. Romans 7:2[1] highlights another law at work within our physical bodies, constantly contending against our minds and leading us into captivity under the law of sin. When a Christian's mind becomes consumed with sexual thoughts, it becomes inaccessible to God, hindering the reception of spiritual revelations from the throne room.

This impairs clear thinking, rational decision-making, and sound judgment. It adversely affects your faith, sowing seeds of doubt in God's Word and promises. Sexual fantasies are often employed as a tool by the enemy to drive you toward complete ruin. The devil wants to render you inactive in ministry, your job, and your family. If you have ever seen the movie "Click," it is a perfect analogy for being a bystander in life, watching everything unfold without actively participating.

Chapter One: Understanding Sexual Fantasy

As vulnerability sets in, it becomes easier for negative influences to push you towards harmful habits like heavy drinking, smoking, or engaging in unhealthy relationships with multiple sexual partners. The underlying goal is to lure you away from God by any means necessary. He wants to entrap your soul, leaving you hell bound.

Signs of Sexual Fantasies

Recognizing if you are struggling with sexual fantasies can be complex, as thoughts are internal and not always visible. However, some potential signs and behaviors may indicate such a struggle. Remember that these signs are not definitive proof. If you suspect you are struggling with signs of sexual fantasies, it is essential to approach the situation with fasting, prayer, and spiritual deliverance.

- **Mood Swings:** Frequent mood swings, anxiety, guilt, or depression could be signs of internal turmoil related to sexual fantasies.

- **Change in Behavior:** A sudden behavior change, such as becoming secretive or exhibiting unusual habits, could suggest you are dealing with internal conflicts.

- **Excessive Internet Usage:** If you excessively engage with sexually explicit content such as online porn, this could indicate a struggle with sexual fantasies.

- **Avoiding Certain Topics:** You avoid conversations about relationships, intimacy, or sexuality, possibly because these discussions will trigger your inner struggles.

Sexual Fantasy & The Christian Mind

- **Disrupted Sleep Patterns:** Persistent difficulty falling asleep or experiencing nightmares might indicate unresolved issues, including sexual fantasies.

- **Decreased Spiritual Involvement:** A decreased engagement in attending church events. Broken fellowship with church leaders, spiritual parents, friends who can see in the spirit realm, or spiritual mentors. This might suggest that you feel disconnected due to your inner struggles.

- **Change in Dress or Appearance:** Sudden changes in dress or appearance might indicate a desire for attention or validation related to your fantasies- an overwhelming urge to wear tight or revealing clothing.

  Changes in Emotional Expression: Heightened altered emotional reactions when discussing sexuality, intimacy, or relationships. It makes you uncomfortable out of fear of your hidden sins being revealed.

- **Self-Esteem Issues:** Feelings of low self-esteem and body image issues that lead to rejection and self-rejection. Listening to the lies of the enemy that your body is not good enough and you should do something to augment your appearance

Chapter One: Understanding Sexual Fantasy

It is important to note that all sexual fantasies are inherently harmful, in the Christian mind, and can lead to individuals having sexual dreams that interfere with their spiritual well-being. Relationships, or values—addressing these feelings and seeking guidance, such as fervent prayer, open conversations, or spiritual support, is beneficial in keeping you in right standing with God.

CHAPTER TWO
THE PURPOSE OF SEXUAL FANTASIES
The Erotic Mind

How, can Christians navigate the complexities of desire? Reconciling the intricacies of their fantasies with their faith commitments. This chapter gives insight into proposing a structure for exploring self-discovery, reconciliation, and flourishing in your faith and sexuality. You have grace as a believer, but God's grace may not always abound, especially when you keep repeating the cycle of sin instead of ending it. Yes, you may have a human desire for sex, but you have the power within you to bring your flesh under subjection. Unlawful sex brings you to a place of spiritual ruin, you wake up tired in the morning because your mind has been traveling all night.

You had sex in Dubai, Mexico, the shores of Jamaica, and Hawaii, just to name a few. An erotic mind is always on the move. In the past, Christians were encouraged to be modest and humble. This applied to all areas of their lives. Who or what is behind a Christian believer going against the will of God by entertaining impure sexual thoughts in their mind? The phrase "this is not your grandmother's gospel" may cause some of you to come unhinged, but it remains true there was a time when a sinner driving by a church would turn their music down out of fear and reverence for God. Now, Christians are entering the church parking lot with gospel rap blaring on Sunday morning.

Sexual Fantasy & The Christian Mind

The modern-day Christian believes in serving God on their terms, which is rooted in disobedience, this creates a thin line between holy and unholy. They often desire the blessings of God more than his discipline. This behavior opens the door for the devil to get into their minds. The Christian mindset is meant to focus on things that are *"pure, honest, just, lovely, true, and of good report"*[1] (Phil. 4.8), rather than dwelling on lust, sexual fantasies, and impure thoughts. Their range of ungodly thinking spans from those who view desire as a path to deeper spiritual comprehension to others who see it as a potential moral hazard.

Understanding how Christians think about sexuality requires a journey through the historical development of Christian perspectives. The Christian mind is a dynamic entity shaped by numerous factors, and the goal in exploring this is not to lump everyone's views together but to recognize the diverse beliefs within the faith. Throughout the history of Christianity, attitudes toward the body, sex, and desire have taken various forms, showcasing a continuous evolution in the way believers maneuver their humanity.

Cultural Influences

Our identities as Christians are not molded in isolation but are deeply entwined with the cultural nuances in which we find ourselves. Broader cultural narratives shape our understanding of desire, influencing how we perceive our fantasies and navigate the interplay between faith and sexuality. In contemporary culture, where tension between liberation and restraint often marks conversations about sex, the Christian mind is exposed to a myriad of cultural influences. Media representations, societal expectations, and prevailing attitudes toward sex contribute to the lens through which Christians view their desires.

Chapter Two: The Purpose of Sexual Fantasies

Piloting the intersection of cultural impacts and the Christian identity is essential. By critically examining these influences, we can discern how cultural contexts may contribute to the Christian mind's approach to sexual fantasies and explore avenues for a more intentional and authentic Christian identity within contemporary culture.

THE CHRISTIAN MIND AND SEXUALITY

The purpose of sexual fantasies in the life of a believer is to separate you from God by corrupting your mind. Isaiah 59:2-15 reads, *your "iniquities have separated you from your God, and your sins have hidden His face from you so that He will not hear. For your hands are defiled with blood, and your fingers with iniquity; Your lips have spoken lies, your tongue has muttered perversity."*[1] God wants you to be separated from the world but not from him. The devil wants you to be connected to your flesh when engaging in the things of the world. This will isolate you from God by sending you into hiding (Genesis 3:8).[1] Your mind is the battlefield for the enemy.

> *"Finally, be strong in the Lord and the power of his might. Put on the full armor of God, that you may be able to stand firm against the schemes of the devil.* Ephesians 6:10-18.[1]

There is no need to put on the armor of God in the morning if you are going to allow the devil to take your clothes off in the evening. Your mind is the engine that controls your entire body. If you continue to let your mind be clogged with immoral sexual thoughts, it will destroy your spirit.

Sexual Fantasy & The Christian Mind

An erotic mind develops over time and where your mind goes, your body follows. As a Christian, you are charged to *"set your affection on things above, not on things on the earth. For ye are dead, and your life is hidden with Christ in God. When Christ, who is our life, shall appear, then shall ye also appear with him in glory"* (Colossians 3:2).[1]

Another purpose of sexual perversion is to remove God's glory from your life and affect your ability to work in ministry. It is tough to execute the will of God concerning you when you are waist-deep (literally) in unlawful sexual acts. *"For the gifts and calling of God are without repentance"* (Rom. 11.29).[1] Your gifts will continue to operate even in a sinful state, though not in their purest form. It will be hit-or-miss until you repent and return to God. Like it or not, you are engulfed in a war of good and evil. Time is winding up, and the enemy is not giving up without a fight.

He is playing for keeps, sex is one of the most effective tools in his arsenal. The weapon of sex creates soul ties. Other methods of sin may claim a few souls here and there for the kingdom of darkness, but a soul tie gives him the big win. It allows him to claim many souls in a short period. A soul tie is a connection with someone deeply embedded into your soul.[2] Often, it is thought of as a sexual connection, but it can also be formed in the realm of close friendship. A soul tie is a profound connection with another person that becomes deeply intertwined with your inner being.[2]

This connection is often associated with intimate relationships, with some believing that it can form particularly after engaging in sexual activity with someone. Every person you have sex with accessing their soul puts you in relatedness with all the souls of the people they have had sex with, and so on.[2] This creates entangled roots, which will make it more challenging to break free when you seek deliverance from the spirit associated with sexual perversion.

Chapter Two: The Purpose of Sexual Fantasies

Spiritual soul ties will block you from having true intimacy with God. It will impair your ability to worship him in spirit and truth (John 4:24).[1] An erotic mind is a carnal mind that will not allow you to comprehend or process the things of God.

"For those who live according to the flesh set their minds on the things of the flesh, but those who live according to the spirit. The things of the spirit, for to be carnally minded is death, but to be spiritually minded is life and peace. Because the carnal mind is enmity against God: for it is not subject to the law of God, neither indeed can be. So, then they that are in the flesh cannot please God" (Romans 8:6-8).[1]

Living under the influence of an erotic mind creates chaos in your life. This mindset makes it difficult for you to experience the peace of God. The erotic feeling of sexual fantasies lasts temporarily. The sensations only persist as long as you are entertaining the thoughts in your mind. However, once the thoughts cease you are left feeling like a toxic wasteland. You feel disgusted and ashamed. Nevertheless, God's peace will surpass your natural understanding (Philippians 4:7).[1] Having God's peace protects your heart and mind in Christ Jesus and will lift up a standard against the enemy. Sexual perversion comes into your life to eradicate every spiritual seed that was planted in your mind by God for growth and spiritual development. These Godly seeds are conducive to your maturity and survival as a Christian.

THE EFFECTS OF AN EXOTIC MIND

An exotic mind is Anything of foreign origin, something not of native growth, such as a plant, a word, or a custom.[3] Sexual fantasies are designed to alter the inner workings of your mind. It starts by creating a comfort zone each time you engage in this imagery.

It feels like a safe space for you to express the suppressed portions of your sexual desire. It relieves stress by catapulting you into an alternate reality of existence. This alternate reality allows you to be the person you want to be instead of the person you are. There is a weight to being a responsible individual, and for some of you, life feels overwhelming. Entering the land of fantasy allows you to breathe. As comforting as it may feel, sin is still sin, and once it is produced, the fruit of it is death. God will give you space to repent, but if you ignore his nudges, sin will take you in a downward direction of erotica to a foreign place in your mind. The sin of sexual fantasies will work to rob you of your sanity.

THE SEXUAL SIN OF KING HEROD (MATTEW 6:14-29)[1]

King Herod Antipas[4] wanted to marry Herodias, his half-brother, Philip's wife however, this desire was opposed by John the Baptist. According to the Mosaic law (Leviticus 18:12),[1] it was unlawful for him to be with her. Firstly, Herodias was his half-cousin—the daughter of his half-uncle. Secondly, she was married to his half-brother Philip, which in turn made her his sister-in-law. In addition, Philip had male heirs with his wife and was still alive. The elders would have considered the marriage feasible if Philip was dead with no male heirs (Deuteronomy 25:5-10).[1] Thirdly, both Herodias and Herod would need to divorce their respective spouses to get married to each other.

King Herod's wife, Phasaelis, was the daughter of an Arabian king. In those days, divorcing royalty was considered an insult that could result in a war between two kingdoms.[4] Herod wanted to kill John the Baptist because he refused to stop preaching against him being with the woman after whom he was lusting. Herod, however, feared the people's reaction because they esteemed John to be a prophet.

Chapter Two: The Purpose of Sexual Fantasies

On the night of his birthday celebration, his niece—Herodias and Philip's daughter—danced for him and all his guests, verse 22 reads that her dancing pleased him so much "The King said to the **girl**, ask me for anything you want, and I'll give it to you." He promised to give her anything that she asked for. Heeding her mother's advice, she asked for the head of John the Baptist on a platter, which he obliged. Theologians speculate the young girl was between the ages of twelve and fourteen. They are uncertain as to why he was so pleased with her dancing that he would offer whatever she desired.[5] This is what the kingdom of sexual perversion does to a person. It claims the life of the innocent and the young, King Herod may have fantasized about his niece sexually during her performance.

We already know this is a man who does not adhere to the laws of God, so what would have stopped him from wanting the mother and the daughter? He was already deep in incestuous practices. Herodias had to be a woman of great beauty. He ruined the familial relationship with his half-brother and destroyed an entire kingdom just to have her. He divorced his current wife and married Herodias, which started a war he eventually lost thus leading to his exile to Gaul, where he died of gangrene of the genitalia. This King Herod should not be confused with the one in the Book of Acts, that is his grandson.

The intensity behind an erotic mind leads you to crave sexual experiences you have never encountered before because it is self-centered and selfish. These are the desires that cause many to lose everything including their lives.

FANTASY AND THE MIND

The human mind is a powerful and complicated creation. It is where dreams are born and nurtured. While some stories can be positive and enhance intimacy within the context of marriage, others might be unhealthy or counterproductive if you are single.

Sexual Fantasy & The Christian Mind

In Philippians 4:8, the apostle Paul instructs believers, *"Finally, brothers and sisters, whatever is true, whatever is noble, whatever is right, whatever is pure, whatever is lovely, whatever is admirable—if anything is excellent or praiseworthy—think about such things."* [1]

This scripture encourages you to filter your thoughts through the lens of godly virtues. Sexual fantasy caused King Herod's mind to enter a place of profound desires and imaginative mastery after watching his niece dance. His mind became fertile ground where boundaries blur, in the realm of erotic fantasy. It is a playground where the imagination knows no bounds, allowing you to experiment with different roles, scenarios, and sensations that will lead you down a dark path of lust and worldly desires. This space in your mind is free to explore the depths of arousal, indulging in scenes that may be unattainable or forbidden in reality.

Furthermore, your mind's capacity to conjure elaborate fantasies reveals the sophisticated connection between your thoughts and physical responses. As you immerse yourselves in your fantasies, your bodies respond in kind, igniting a cascade of sensations that can rival the intensity of any physical touch. Sexual fantasy in the mind of a devout believer is a delicate subject, often influenced by your individual religious beliefs, morals, values, and cultural upbringing.

For someone who holds strong religious convictions, sexual fantasies may be approached with caution and introspection. God is not the one sending you these fantasies. Sexual imagery of the mind takes on a different tone when you discover this is hell's agenda to keep you connected to the things of the flesh.

Sexual fantasies may be filtered through the lens of morality and spirituality, with a desire to align them with the teachings of your faith. Some of you may find yourselves fighting with the notion of whether specific fantasies are acceptable or sinful according to your religious doctrine.

Chapter Two: The Purpose of Sexual Fantasies

Sexual fantasies in the mind of a believer are wrong in the sight of God and will take you to a place of demonic dimension in the spirit. The erotic mind of a devout believer in the realm of sexual fantasies may evoke feelings of guilt and conflict. Fantasies may take on a deeply personal and intimate quality in this realm of exploration. Escaping the entrapment of your mind will require a deeper understanding of the profound connection that binds you to the seasonal cycle of sexual perversion.

SEXUAL FANTASIES AND THE SINGLE CHRISTIAN

The exploration of sexual fantasies becomes a more multifaceted matter for single Christians, while God's design for sexual expression is primarily within the bounds of marriage, the reality is that single Christians still experience sexual desires. You must approach sexual fantasies with self-awareness and discernment.

1 Corinthians 6:19-20 reminds us, *"Do you not know that your bodies are temples of the Holy Spirit, who is in you, whom you have received from God? You are not your own; you were bought at a price. Therefore, honor God with your bodies."*[1]

This verse tells singles to treat their bodies and minds as sacred spaces that belong to God. Understanding the purpose of sexual fantasies can help you manage your role in life. God designed sex to be a unifying and pleasurable experience for couples within the composition of marriage. In the Songs of Solomon, we find poetic descriptions of marital intimacy that celebrate the beauty of physical touch between a man and his wife. Fantasies that are shared openly and respectfully within the marital relationship can strengthen the emotional and physical bond between partners.

Sexual Fantasy & The Christian Mind

SEXUAL FANTASIES AND THE MARRIED CHRISTIAN

"Jump in, let's do this! It's time for some nasty, toe-curling, spank me, lick me, no holds bar lawless sex." That is your expectation as you peeled back the covers and climbed into bed with your spouse on your honeymoon. Once in the bed, they lean in close to you, and you move in closer to them, both of you gaze into each other's eyes as your lips connect for a kiss. It was a little awkward, but overall, not bad. Your hands start moving, and the clothing comes off, five minutes later, it is over. Leaving one of you lying there with the covers pulled up to your neck. Wondering what just occurred and how it happened so fast. You lie there, trying to maintain your composure. After all, arguing on your wedding night is not ideal, especially about sex; that is the last thing you want to do. But as you replay the encounter in your mind.

Out of nowhere, you hear a stern voice telling you to touch yourself, your spouse did not satisfy you, so now you must take matters into your own hands. At first, you resist, but then the voice uses scripture against you: *"The married bed is undefiled."* Hebrews 13:4-6. [1] When the scripture does not work, the devil then opens the floodgate for sexual fantasies by sending image after image to your mind. He then commands you to do it. Feeling scared as if you just signed up for a lifetime of boring sex, you look over to see if your spouse is asleep. Once you confirm they are, you carry out the devil's command. When the act is complete, you are filled with guilt, disgust, and shame.

You then make yourself a promise to never do that again, not realizing you just allowed the adversary into your marriage. You are powerless in reversing this action, as he now possesses a legitimate right to remain in your marriage as a spirit spouse until you cast him out and close the portal that you opened in ignorance.

Chapter Two: The Purpose of Sexual Fantasies

The realm of sexual fantasies is a door opener, and being a married Christian does not exempt you from being attacked by these demonic forces. Once you let them in the first time, they will create sexual strongholds in your marriage that will take you to a place where you enjoy sex more with yourself than with your spouse.

THE DANGERS OF UNRESTRAINED FANTASIES

Sexual fantasies can be used as a form of escapism from the worries of life, but they can also pose risks when left unchecked. Stories involving objectification, exploitation, or illicit behaviors can contribute to dissatisfaction, comparison, and unrealistic relationship expectations. Jesus' words in Matthew 5:28 remind us of the importance of guarding our thoughts: *"But I tell you that anyone who looks at a woman lustfully has already committed adultery with her in his heart."* This principle emphasizes the need to maintain the purity of thought and intention. The practice of fantasy starts by creating the perfect world which spirals out of control.

Over time these illusory images morph into a black hole that sucks you in deeper and deeper until you lose sight of who you are in Christ. The aftermath of sexual fantasies leaves you in a place of hopelessness and mindless confusion.

THE WRONG THOUGHTS

"If these thoughts are wrong, I don't wanna be right." Sexual fantasies offer an escape when life feels overwhelming, providing an opportunity to catch your breath and distance yourself from the difficulties you are facing. Coping with the hurdles of everyday life can be daunting for modern-day Christians, who strive to maintain their spiritual walk with God while confronting numerous obstacles, including the devil.

Sexual Fantasy & The Christian Mind

It is a lot for anyone, and many people deal with it alone, making it even more demanding. Luke 22:31-32 reads, *"Simon, Simon, behold, Satan hath desired to have you, that he may sift you as wheat: But I have prayed for thee, that thy faith fails not: and when thou art converted, strengthen thy brother."*[1]

Who is praying for you amid your siftings? You may feel as if you are fighting these sexual impurities alone, but you are not. This book was written with you in mind, many Christians struggle with feelings of isolation and aloneness. The dynamics of the modern church have changed, the church is more focused on becoming the next mega-church or social media viral sensation. which leaves a lot of believers fending for themselves. This leads to much trial and error as many of you are left in the dark to figure things out on your own.

In pursuing mega-church status, most new-age leaders have done away with the practices that create victorious Christian living and discipleship. This occurred when they discontinued noon-day prayers, early morning prayer lines, revivals, shut-ins, and regular fasting throughout the year. These practices played a pivotal role in keeping Christians engaged and grounded. Being engulfed in sin creates more questions than answers. How did we arrive at this point; where so many Christians are struggling with sexual immorality? What impact does it have on your spiritual walk with God? How can you overcome the urge to fantasize? While you may not have all the answers, take confidence that the Holy Spirit will not leave you comfortless in your quest for deliverance and wholeness.

WHY IS THIS HAPPENING?

When Christians experience sexual fantasies, they often question the reason behind it. "Why" becomes a recurring question that lingers in your thoughts.

Chapter Two: The Purpose of Sexual Fantasies

According to Romans 7:23, *there is another law at work within us, warring against the law of our minds and holding us captive to the law of sin residing within us."*[1] The enemy attacks the mind, launching his fiery darts aimed at your thoughts (Ephesians 6:10).[1] Sexual fantasies is a weapon used by the devil to distort your mind, hindering you from maintaining focus on God and His Word. Sexual fantasies can be a sensitive topic, especially for Christians. The idea of sexual thoughts and desires can weigh heavily on the conscience of those who strive to live a holy life and uphold their faith.

For many Christians, these fantasies can be a source of shame and guilt, leading to feelings of isolation and despair. It is a topic often avoided or dismissed, yet it is a prevalent issue affecting many believers. Exploring the root causes of these thoughts and their impact on your spiritual walk with God will lead you to the long-term deliverance you seek.

SEXUAL FANTASIES AND THE MIND OF A CHRISTIAN

It is essential to acknowledge that sexual fantasies are a part of human nature. They exist in the minds of people of all faiths and backgrounds, and Christians are no exception. However, the shame and guilt associated with these thoughts can be overwhelming for a lot of believers. This shame can lead to feelings of separation, and many Christians find it daunting to seek assistance or direction on coping with such thoughts. Indulging in sexual fantasies can open spiritual doors that may lead to sinful acts. While such stories may start innocently, they can spiral out of control over time and become increasingly unethical.

Sexual Fantasy & The Christian Mind

Sexual fantasies can hold you captive in your mind, creating a brain fog that makes it arduous to function in your everyday life. The clouding of consciousness that you are experiencing can be attributed to the squid and the octopus spirits.[6] They are a part of the Marine Kingdom and work in conjunction with the spirit of sexual perversion; these are all mind-controlling spirits whose job is to keep you in a daze, leaving you confused. According to Matthew 15:19,[1] wicked thoughts such as murder, adultery, theft, false testimony, and slander, originate from the heart. Although sexual thoughts initially arise in the mind, if entertained and nurtured, eventually, they will take root in your heart.

The adversary aims to tempt you into acting upon your fantasies, whether they are sexual or otherwise, ultimately leading to immoral behavior. These fantasies can become problematic when they interfere with your daily life or spiritual walk with God. Therefore, discussing how to manage these thoughts in a healthy way that honors God is essential. Your job as Christians is to "*cast down imaginations, and every high thing that exalted itself against the knowledge of God and bringing into captivity every thought to the obedience of Christ*" 2 Corinthians 10:5.[1] Vain imaginations lead believers away from the will of God. Allowing impure thoughts to dominate your mind, corrupt your dreams, and block your visions. Many Christians lose the ability to remember their dreams because of these fantasies.

Chapter Two: The Purpose of Sexual Fantasies

THE SENSITIVE TOPIC OF SEXUAL FANTASIES

The kingdom of darkness operates in a hierarchy. Each time you advance in sin, it opens you up to more spiritual attacks. Sexual fantasy starts in your mind, and then it moves to your emotions. Given time, it creates enough sexual tension and pressure in your body to advance you into self-touch (also known as masturbation). Once you start to masturbate, you open spiritual portals, giving the spirit of sexual perversion direct access to create generational curses in your bloodline. The enemy now has a legal right to launch an attack on the members of your household.

His next step is to get you to commit fornication and adultery and then open you up to having multiple sex partners. You possess the power to terminate these fantasies at will, but if you continue to yield to these thoughts, they will overpower you. Unwittingly, the urge to daydream becomes more pervasive, with each passing moment, you progress deeper into the abyss of darkness, and the adversary uses this opportunity to promote you to a higher level of depravity. Your desire for physical intimacy escalates as you give in to these mental images. This can lead to inappropriate attractions. It may even lead to same-sex interactions.

Unfortunately, your longing for sex will turn your fantasies into reality, outweighing your dedication to moral principles. This marks the beginning of your descent into the depths of sexual deviation. Sexual fantasies and the mind of a Christian began as a thought, but with time, you may find yourself acting out the scenarios in your mind. This is a process that requires a series of steps to be completed. The timeline for this progression can span from a few months to years, contingent upon how quickly the adversary exploits your vulnerabilities.

LET US EXAMINE SOME OF THE STEPS THAT CAN LEAD TO SEXUAL FANTASIES.

- **Escapism:** Yielding to an intense desire to construct an alternate reality to escape your current circumstances.

- **Exposure to sexual content**: Exposure to sexual content through media, conversations, or personal experiences can initiate the thought process of sexual fantasies.

- **Entertaining thoughts:** Continuously dwelling on sexual thoughts, replaying sexual scenes, and imagining new scenarios can further stimulate the mind and ignite sexual fantasies.

- **Justification and rationalization:** Rationalizing sexual fantasies as harmless or justifiable within the context of personal circumstances or beliefs can weaken resistance to the temptation of acting them out.

- **Acting on the fantasies:** Eventually, acting on sexual fantasies could become a reality through self-pleasure or engaging in sexual activities with another person.

- **Guilt and shame:** A Christian may experience guilt and shame after acting on the fantasies, leading to further distress and emotional conflict.

Chapter Two: The Purpose of Sexual Fantasies

These steps may not be the same for everyone; seeking professional guidance and support from a trusted source may help address this issue. You may have become ensnared in the trap of sexual fantasies. Despite seeking deliverance that has proved futile, there is still hope for your salvation; it is possible to break free from sexual sin.

"Therefore, since we are surrounded by such a great cloud of witnesses, let us throw off everything that hinders and the sin that so easily entangles. And let us run with perseverance the race marked out for us" (Romans 12:1).[1]

If you are serious about breaking free from sexual fantasies and their damaging effects on your life, this is one of the most important scriptures you will need to meditate on day and night. You serve a holy God who will not allow sin in any form to dwell in his presence. The world may permit you to be an indecisive Christian, but God does not, and it is reflected in his word from Genesis to Revelation. This is the determining factor in equipping yourself with the knowledge necessary to maintain your spiritual liberty in Christ. Sexual fantasies in the mind of a Christian are regarded as a sensitive topic due to the perception of it being a forbidden subject within religious sectors.

This is comparable to parents who are reluctant to discuss sex with their children, and similarly, the topic of sex is often avoided among like-minded believers within Christianity. This reluctance has resulted in a significant number of Christians suffering in silence. Sexual fantasies are the mental gateway of addiction to sexual immorality.

"For this is the will of God, your sanctification: that you abstain from sexual immorality; that each of you knows how to control his own body in holiness and honor"
1 Thessalonians 4:3-4

CHAPTER THREE
CHILDHOOD & SEXUALITY
How were you introduced to sex?

Welcome to Chapter Three where we will explore the realm of childhood and sexuality. Many individuals struggle with unhealthy connections to sex, this is primarily influenced by the way they were initially introduced to the topic. Some of you were warned against it with notions of it being nasty and could potentially lead to teen pregnancy or contracting sexually transmitted diseases. Others may have experienced reprimands and rebukes and felt ashamed for simply expressing curiosity about sex. Despite the prevalence of sexual imagery in the media, parents still shy away from having open discussions about sex with their children; this approach leaves young people uninformed, which leads them down a path of poor decision-making concerning sex.

In certain households, particularly those with strong Christian beliefs, the word "sex" is seen as taboo or even a curse word. The initial twelve years of a child's life are profoundly influential. During this period, their brain rapidly absorbs and processes information. If parents neglect to furnish the information required for cultivating a healthy perspective on sex during this time, it may distort an adolescent's view of human sexuality. This may result in inner conflicts in their adult life, leaving them to struggle with issues like lust, sexual addiction, impure thoughts, consumption of pornographic content, masturbation, sexual fantasies, or concerns related to body image.

Sexual Fantasy & The Christian Mind

These challenges can be indicative of an unhealthy perception of sex. Gaining control over these issues requires a deeper look into the root causes impacting your outlook.

HOW WERE YOU INTRODUCED TO SEX?

When did you first encounter the concept of sex? Who influenced this foundation? Understanding both the source and manner of your introduction to sex is essential in comprehending its impact on your life. The motives behind their intentions become an essential factor, for instance, if a young man loses his virginity to an older woman, it could lead to a perverted perspective. The older woman may plant harmful seeds in his mind, convincing him that sex is only enjoyable when explored with a mature partner. This encounter may leave him feeling empowered as if he has reached "grown man" status due to the age difference.

This example illustrates how the young man was led into misguided thinking by an older woman operating under the influence of sexual perversion, immaturity, and sexual misconduct. He was essentially seduced into a harmful mindset. While some people may have preferences in their relationships, there is a clear distinction when it comes to crossing ethical boundaries solely for sexual satisfaction. If the roles were reversed, and it was a young woman in this scenario, society would likely label the experience as statutory rape. Using sexism to set ethical boundaries perpetuates the cycle of sexual improprieties among today's youth.

Chapter Three: Childhood & Sexuality

This emphasizes the significance of contemplating your past experiences, especially considering how and by whom you first encountered the concept of sexuality. At what age did you have your first sexual encounter? If this act occurred before your brain's cognitive development, typically around the age of twenty. It had significant consequences on your perception of God's purpose for sex in the earth. Whether consensual or nonconsensual, engaging in sexual activities during adolescence is a carefully orchestrated initiation into the realm of darkness constructed by the devil to ensnare your soul.

Once your soul is captured, a demon guardian (spirit spouse) of darkness is assigned to watch over you. The devil aims to get you to engage in more illicit sexual acts, which, over time, will fragment your soul. Eventually, this will make it harder for you to get delivered from the spirit of sexual perversion. The devil operates on the same concepts as credit card companies, he calls you while you are young to create long-term loyalty while hitting you with erroneous interest charges, making it difficult for you to pay off the balance. But here is the good news if you are ready to get delivered from this sin, JESUS has already paid it all!

God will zero out your balance when you confess with your mouth the Lord Jesus and shall believe in your heart that God has raised him from the dead, you will be saved (Romans 10:9).[1] Sexual intimacy is intended for the married bed, and engaging in sexual endeavors outside of this commitment is deemed unlawful in God's sight. Each time you participate in illicit sexual activities it results in the fragmentation of your soul as you are inviting new spirits into the core of your existence. These spirits claim a part of you, knowing that it will take you years to reconstruct the pieces of your soul that are fragmented.

Sexual Fantasy & The Christian Mind

Even after experiencing a spiritual rebirth, you will find yourself on a quest for answers. Trapped on an emotional roller coaster, eagerly anticipating complete deliverance from the pain of your past. Seeking support from spiritual leaders, therapists, or trusted individuals will be instrumental in your journey toward wholeness.

Utilize the following list to discern whether your soul is fragmented: Remember, identifying these signs is the first step toward your healing and deliverance.

- **Persistent Emotional Turmoil:** If you find yourself frequently experiencing intense emotional highs and lows.

- **Unresolved Past Trauma:** Lingering pain and unresolved trauma from your past can indicate soul fragmentation as the wounds continue to impact your emotional well-being.

- **Repetitive Negative Patterns:** Continuously engaging in self-destructive or harmful behavior patterns may indicate fragmented aspects of your soul influencing your actions.

- **Inability to Form Meaningful Connections:** Challenges in forming deep, meaningful connections with others may signal that certain parts of your soul hinder establishing genuine relationships.

- **Feelings of Emptiness or Numbness:** A pervasive sense of emptiness or emotional numbness may imply that essential parts of your soul are disconnected or inaccessible.

Chapter Three: Childhood & Sexuality

- **Spiritual Disconnect:** If you sense a disconnection from your spiritual self, even after receiving Jesus as your Lord and Savior, it could indicate fragmented aspects of your soul that need attention.

- **Persistent Inner Conflict:** Ongoing internal battles or conflicting thoughts and feelings might be a manifestation of a fragmented soul struggling to find unity.

- **Loss of Joy and Passion:** A consistent absence of joy, passion, or enthusiasm for life may suggest that vital components of your soul need to be fully engaged and present.

- **Difficulty in Forgiving Yourself:** If you find it challenging to forgive yourself for past mistakes or transgressions, it may be an indication of unresolved issues within your soul.

- **Failure:** Everything that you do results in failure instead of success. The enemy has the legal right to keep you locked in a cycle of failure to frustrate your soul.

If you identify with any of these signs, please remember that all is not lost. God's will for your life is for you to be whole and complete, nothing broken and nothing missing (Isaiah 26:3-4).[1] You serve a God who specializes in gathering the fragments; your soul is no exception. *"For the Lord, he is your shepherd; you shall not want. He created you to lie down in green pastures: he leadeth you beside still waters. He **restoreth** your soul: he is leading you in the path of righteousness for his name's sake"* (Ps. 23.1-3).[1] The father wants to put you back together again, open up and let him in. Give him full access to all of you with no limitations.

Sexual Fantasy & The Christian Mind

HOW DID YOU LOSE YOUR VIRGINITY?

How you lost your virginity aids in forming your opinion of sex. If you shared your first experience with a high school sweetheart, it left you feeling empowered because you shared something of value with someone you loved. If you suffered any form of childhood molestation, you may perceive sex as both a pleasure and a torment because what you valued most was taken from you against your will. Even after your molester has been eradicated from your life, you continue in their pattern of behavior by molesting yourself. This happens by way of chronic masturbation as well as having multiple sexual partners, many of whom turned out to be either toxic lovers or abusers.

Until complete deliverance takes place in your mind, you are susceptible to listening to the broken record of lies playing in your mind, telling you that you got what you deserved and that God does not love you. If he did, this would not have happened to you. The enemy's goal is to get to you before God does, sexual molestation often occurs during the impressionable years of a child's life. This happens during the tender years to damage the psyche and get you to develop a dark outlook on life. Most people who experience sexual trauma at a young age often find themselves asking God, "Why did he allow it to happen?" But is it God who allowed this to happen?

Or can it be attributed to poor parenting, lack of guardianship, negligence, and the free will of humanity? If childhood abuse was something that God allowed. Why is it not mentioned in the Bible? Carrying around past hurts and living a life limited by the pain of yesterday is not your portion. The person who violated you had a choice to make, and unfortunately, they made the wrong one. Nevertheless, starting today, you can take your power back by choosing to let go of past trauma by breaking free of the mental prison they locked you in when they hurt you.

Chapter Three: Childhood & Sexuality

Do not allow the promise of a brighter, better future to pay for the pain of yesterday by remaining in a place of stuck. In 2 Samuel 9:7-8, King David searched for a surviving heir of his close friend Jonathan. He made a covenant with his friend to care for his living spouse or children to ensure they never experience lack. King David was told that Jonathan's son Mephibosheth was still alive, but he sustained an injury the day his father died. His caregiver dropped him while she was running to hide him from military personnel whom she thought were approaching to kill him.

In her haste to get him to safety, she fell with the child in her arms, which broke his legs and left him crippled. He was now a grown man who was stuck dealing with past trauma. He was reminded daily of his limitations because he suffered a nasty fall at the hands of his caregiver. When King David located the young man, he spoke kindly to him and told him he wanted him to live with him in the palace. He told him about the promise he made to his father Jonathan, King David even told him not to be afraid. He told him that he would give him the land that belonged to his grandfather, King Saul, and he would always eat at his table.

Instead of getting excited and thanking the King, Mephibosheth bowed down and said (in verse 8), *"What is your servant that you should notice a dead dog like me."* Wow! He referred to himself as a "dead dog." The pain of his past had him in a dead place. It was killing his mind and his body. He had more royal blood in him than the one talking to him, but he was never taught the value of his name. Does this sound like you? The king of glory is giving you an invitation to come and live in his palace so you can eat forever more at his table, but instead of accepting his invitation. You are busy telling God how unworthy you are, you would rather feast on the lies of the devil than embrace God's goodness.

Sexual Fantasy & The Christian Mind

Just like Mephibosheth, your guardian dropped you. Now, you find yourself living with the aftermath of their actions, your present-day brokenness has left you fighting a battle in your mind. The cycle of sexual immortality you are trying to overcome is not yours it has been passed down the family bloodline like an heirloom. This is why it goes away for a season and then returns stronger than before. Someone in your bloodline entered a covenant of sexual perversion with the devil either by way of witchcraft or committing impure sexual acts with kids, the occult, bestiality, or getting married to a spirit spouse. Until you break this curse, the enemy has the legal right to sexually molest you, your spouse, your children, and future generations.

THE FATHERLESS CHILD

A woman who grew up without a father in the home may find herself gravitating towards older men. This stems from unresolved "Daddy issues." The affection you feel for these men serves as a coping mechanism to compensate for the abandonment you experienced from your father. This type of relationship typically does not last because once they discover you are suffering from daddy issues, they want no part of it. Their departure reignites the sting of your original rejection experienced during the initial abandonment of your father. After their exit, you suffer with the pain of nostalgia from the recollection of that unfaithful day when your father walked away.

The stabbing pain in your chest, the shortness of breath, it all comes rushing back to you. Memories of all the countless times he promised to take you out for ice cream after he left, flood your mind. He told your mom to get you dressed because he was coming to pick you up. She was excited at the prospect of your father spending time with you. So, she dressed you in a white dress, styled your hair into two ponytails with a bow, and sat you on the front step where you waited patiently for hours.

Chapter Three: Childhood & Sexuality

But your dad never came. Now, as an adult, your mind is still sitting on the front steps waiting for your Dad, who never showed up. The search for the man who will step in and play the role of your father continues as you date older men, hoping that one of them will rescue the little girl within. Some of you are married and find yourself being mean to your husband, using him as a scapegoat, wanting him to pay for the pain your father inflicted. You randomly lash out at your husband, saying hurtful things like, "You are never there for me" or "You never protect me." You do not have to remain trapped in this cycle of pain where you hide behind a mask of perfectionism while struggling to maintain your connection with God, finding yourself slipping in and out of fellowship with him.

One minute you are in the church body, the next you are out of the body. Remember Psalm 27:10, *"When my father and my mother forsake me, then the Lord will take me up."*[1] The day your natural father rejected you, God was there with his arms wide open. He is still waiting for you to stop pretending you are okay and let him in so he can mend your broken heart. When you forgive your dad and everyone else who hurt you, God's love will fill your heart like a mighty rushing wind (Acts 2:1-4).[1] He will do a suddenly in your life. The absence of a father's love, paired with his rejection, can be maddening to a young child. The deep impact of this level of rejection followed you into adulthood and almost drove you crazy.

But God intervened, and because of his intervention, you survived. Stop seeking validation from these older men by giving them your body because you are craving the love and affection of your birth father. End the cycle of sexual misconduct, accept God as your father, and live! Some males struggle with same-sex attraction due to an inner yearning to establish a connection with their father. Your mind is stuck at the age of abandonment, leading you to live a life void of male guidance and masculinity.

Sexual Fantasy & The Christian Mind

God called you to be a vessel of honor, not dishonor, it is time for you to stop being a secret agent for the devil. Outwardly, you appear to be a child of God, but inwardly, you are dying from your strange sexual endeavors. Romans 1:26-28 reads,

"For this reason, God gave them up to dishonorable passions. For their women exchanged natural relations for those that are contrary to nature, and the men likewise gave up natural relations with women and were consumed with passion for one another, men committing shameless acts with men and receiving in themselves the due penalty for their error. And since they did not see fit to acknowledge God, God gave them up to a debased mind to do what ought not to be done."[1]

Your father chose not to be a part of your life for reasons unknown to you. Stop blaming yourself for his decision. Let God heal you from the pain caused by your father's absence. Remember, your father's actions are not worth you suffering for all eternity in hell. On the opposite end of the spectrum, some men exhibit arrogance and narcissism in their masculinity. This lack of witnessing genuine love and protection in their lives has left them unable to truly love and protect a woman. Consequently, they adopt a more dogmatic approach when interacting with the opposite sex. While they may provide for their families, they remain emotionally unavailable, unable to access their feelings due to the anguish of being a "rejected son."

This emotional barrier causes complications in communication, leading them to shut down and shut others out, operating from a place of selfishness with little regard for others' feelings. Their arrogance makes them susceptible to the snares of the enemy, leading them to watch porn, masturbate, and use women for sexual pleasures as a means of numbing their pain. Even as a born-again believer, they lack genuine fear and reverence for God and his people, treating them with disregard.

Chapter Three: Childhood & Sexuality

MIDDLE SCHOOL DAYS

Grades six through eight mark a pivotal time in a child's adolescence. During this stage, they are barraged with emotions and hormonal changes. This is also the mean phase of their life that leads to teasing and bullying. This behavior helps them separate social classes within the student body. Once it is determined who is cool vs. uncool, the next step is to make a spectacle of the fat, nerdy, weird, odd, ugly duckling-looking kids. Receiving such teasing during this stage of development can have a detrimental impact leading into adulthood. If you fell into one or more of these categories, you were a late bloomer who one day woke up and discovered that you went from yuck to yum according to the standards of the social hierarchy.

This shift in societal acceptance has influenced your perspective on interacting with individuals of the opposite sex. For some, this leads to tendencies that hinder faithfulness in both natural and spiritual relationships. This shift in your physical attributes heightened your preoccupation with how you looked, leading you to idolize your new appearance. This change affected your relationship with God resulting in a lack of Time for spiritual pursuits as your focus turned toward maintaining your physicality.

Colossians 3:5 reads. *"Put to death, therefore, whatever belongs to your earthly nature: sexual immorality, impurity, lust, evil desires, and greed, which is* **idolatry.**"[1]

The worshipping of one's self-image opens doors to sexual fantasies. Armed with a new body and good looks, who on earth can resist you? This erroneous thinking is sure to take you down a path of having exciting, mindless mental sex with yourself until it manifests into your reality to include someone else. Repent, ask God for forgiveness, and turn back to God with your whole heart worshipping your appearance is vanity.

On the flip side of things, the teasing and bullying drove some of you into a mental cave that left you feeling invisible. This became your method of coping by giving you a way of escape. Given time, the isolation of being alone taught you how to create an alternate world for you to exist in. What started as an innocent safe space soon opened portals of darkness that led straight to the demonic realm of lust and sexual fantasy. This eventually led you down a path of masturbation, and with each climax, you felt visible and empowered. You finally felt like a man or woman of importance, all the control was in your hand, and you decided when and how you broke yourself off. No one would boss you around or bully you anymore, then one day you felt God tugging at your heart to turn loose the sins of the flesh and be saved.

Now that you have given your life to Christ, breaking free from past behaviors has proven to be a challenge. Each attempt leaves you feeling as if you are at the end of a vacuum; every time you try to escape, the sexual fantasies return to your mind with the intense feelings attached.

"O wretched man that I am, who shall deliver me from this body of death. For the good that I would do, I do it not because evil is present with me" (Romans 7:24-25).[1]

THE FORBIDDEN FRUIT

If you grew up in a home where sex was a taboo topic, your curiosity opened a portal to sexual fantasies by leaving you wondering about the mysteries of sex. Maybe you were not allowed to hang out with friends or family members outside your home. These restrictions turned you into an avid reader of romance novels because they provided a way to escape from your boring reality. These books gave you more than just an escape. They intensified your curiosity about sex by providing steamy sexual scenes that enhanced your imagination.

Chapter Three: Childhood & Sexuality

The words written on the pages felt so real, it left your body feeling hot as you sat there biting your lips and running your hands up and down your thighs while contemplating if you should take it to the next level and finish yourself off. In this moment, the enemy's plan was accomplished in your life. He used the imagery of sexual fantasies described on the pages of a novel to indoctrinate you into a lifestyle of masturbation. Maybe your parents were strict and religious and convinced themselves that keeping you locked in the house was the best way for them to protect you from the outside world. But even amid their attempt to keep you hidden, a flaw in their plan was revealed, and once you discovered that loophole, you took advantage of the opportunity by bringing the sex scenes described on the pages of your novel to life.

The fact that your parents were strict and never let you out of their sight created the fear of missing out on life inside of you. So, the minute you got a little freedom you took it and ran with it. "What do they know anyway? Bunch of bible pushers." Your freedom tasted sweet, and the sex was good or so you thought until you got pregnant or worse. Now, here you are, a grown adult in Christ, facing the same restrictions as when you were young. Being told to abstain from sexual immorality. It feels like you are back at your parents' house all over again. You do good for a few years before literally finding yourself in a compromising position. How do you end this cycle? Keep reading, and you will find the answer.

THE RAPE THAT LEFT YOU SILENT

What is the name of your rapist? The one who tried to rip you out of your right mind. It has been years, and you are still stuck dealing with the aftermath of their actions. As a child, their lewd act sent you into hiding. Their violent indiscretion taught you how to be seen and not heard; it left you afraid to speak up or tell anyone what happened. After all, they told you it was your fault; this was the gateway to your lifelong affair with guilty, nasty, dirty, kinky sex. Spank me, choke me, slap me, pull my hair, whip me, give it to me harder. These are the things you scream while indulging in sexual pleasures, not knowing this is your way of continuing your initial violation. For those of you who were raped by a person of the same sex, the twisted event has thrown your mind into the realm of fetish. Even while being with someone of the opposite sex, you still require them to perform acts as if you are with a same-sex partner. True deliverance will take place when you break your silence. "But I am a child of God and he set me free when he saved me."

The sexual urges you are struggling with are not your own but as long as you remain silent, they will continue to get stronger and stronger. Your secret desires are driving you crazy, and the only escape you have is the world of sexual fantasies. You look forward to going to sleep at night because this is when things get hot and steamy in your mind. Release the name of your rapist and break the soul tie that was formed in you against your will; you can't close what you don't expose. God wants you to enjoy sex within the bonds of marriage, what you experienced was demonic. If you do not allow yourself to be healed from the pain of this sexual trauma. You will attempt to perform these profane sexual acts in your marriage, and it will give the devil the legal right to come in and destroy your home.

DEALING WITH SEXUAL FETISHES

Sexual fetishes speak to unhealthy sexual desires. These perverse inclinations are derived from a sadistic mind that is entirely controlled by demons. Romans 12:1 tells us *"To be ye transformed by renewing our mind."*[1] If this sounds like you, there is hope when you fight your way back to the light. You can get rid of your fetishes by removing everything in your possession that gives this realm access to you. Get rid of the pictures, videos, monthly subscriptions, sex toys, whips, chains, butt plugs, and any other tools that you use for sexual pleasure.

Chapter Three: Childhood & Sexuality

Fetish falls under the category of idolatry because you are worshipping a thing or different parts of the human anatomy.
1 Corinthians 10:14[1] encourages believers to flee from idolatry.

GETTING THE MONKEY OFF YOUR BACK

We have covered a lot in this chapter, but now it is time to talk about the monkey on your back, that makes it hard for you to move forward in God. It is the thing you do late at night that causes your mind to be cloudy and distracted the next day. Matthew 6:22-23 reads, *"The eyes are the windows to your soul, and if your eyes are healthy, your whole body will be filled with light, but if your eyes are unhealthy, then your whole body will be filled with darkness."*[1]

Why do you use your eyes to look at pornography? You do this because, at some point growing up, you were led to believe that watching sexual acts was not the same as engaging in them. Porn, unfortunately, is like a gateway drug. You start in one area, but you find yourself in another. Each time you press play on any pornographic material, it takes over another part of your soul until you find yourself fully involved in the act of chronic masturbation. Self-pleasure is a strong desire that is fueled daily by the sexual fantasies in your mind. Over time, this creates a stronghold, rendering you helpless to the command of demonic spirits who enter your life to promote you in sin.

If you are not careful before you know it, you will find yourself tied up in a sex den with a red ball in your mouth, wondering how you got there while talking to God telepathically, telling him, "Lord, if you get me out of this. I will serve you for the rest of my life." There has been a notable shift in the patterns of porn consumption relating to gender roles over the past decade.

While traditionally, men were predominantly associated with struggles related to porn addiction, there is now a concerning increase in the number of women facing this issue. This change in dynamics can be attributed to shifts in socioeconomic class, the breakdown of traditional family structures, and a rising number of divorces, with more women assuming leadership roles in the home and the workplace, they find themselves seeking ways to relieve stress. Unfortunately, the utilization of porn has become an outlet for escapism to get away from it all. From a spiritual perspective, the spirit of sexual perversion aims to claim generations and to do so, it has to bind the strong man of the house.

Mark 3:27 reads, *"In fact, no one can enter a strong man's house without first tying him up. Then he can plunder the strong man's house."*[1] The United States Census Bureau[2] indicates that mothers lead eighty percent of single-parent households. This implies that the adversary seeks to restrain the women operating as head of household to gain access to the children.

THE ADULT VIEW

God invented sex for a man and woman to become one when they enter a lasting union. But what God meant for good the enemy is using for evil. Although you received erroneous information about sex during your childhood, it is time to change your viewpoint on your perception of intercourse. Experiencing trauma of any kind keeps you stuck at the point of impact. This will deprive you of the mental capacity to see sexual activity from an adult perspective. It causes you to lack a mature understanding of the purpose of Godly sex (yes, there is such a thing).

Chapter Three: Childhood & Sexuality

This is a guilt-free sexual experience that does not leave you feeling dirty afterward or compromised in any way. Now that you are an adult, what have you done to adopt a new mindset as it pertains to human sexuality? Are you still "lining them up" to "knock them down" while telling yourself that God understands? Are you walking in the office of a modern-day Christian who lives in a state of a sexually induced coma? God reserved sex for the married bed, and the more men and women of today refuse to marry, the more the pattern of indulging in illegal coitus continues. This behavior opens a demonic portal for you to create soul ties with a spirit spouse.

Here are the signs to identify if you have a spirit husband or wife.

- A strong overwhelming urge to masturbate.
- Overwhelmed with lust even when reading the Bible or in a church service.
- Refusing to get married but desiring someone else's spouse.
- Not being approached in public because you already appear to be married.
- Strong feeling of a ring on your ring finger
- Refusal to date or get out of the house to be around others.
- Sabotaging relationships/always having dreams that the person you are with is cheating on you.
- You are invisible to the opposite sex.

Sexual Fantasy & The Christian Mind

THE ROOT OF IT ALL

When a child is born, they are sweet and innocent; they know nothing about sex or perversion. So, who taught it to them? Many new parents believe they only need to christen their children and provide for them. That is not the case when engaged in spiritual warfare, they need to do more such as breaking the generational curse of sexual perversion hidden in the bloodline. Here is the short end of it all, the enemy needs a legal right to work in people's lives. Before he attacks, he checks the bloodline to make sure he has the legal right to sexually enslave a person.

Many families carried generational secrets to their graves, leaving the next generation sitting on a faulty line of undisclosed information to figure out what went wrong on their own. This misfortune often leaves individuals in a family structure wondering why they cannot stop the pattern of destructive sexual behavior despite all their efforts to make a change. This is because the spirits you are fighting are not your own, but they are generational. Your ancestor offered up their bloodline as a sacrifice to demon gods. After all, they would not be alive to witness your struggles in trying to live righteously, so why should they care? They allowed the devil to impose a generational curse on future generations in exchange for material wealth. Once the act was complete, their "luck" began changing, and the devil now had a legal right to release the spirit of sexual perversion in their bloodline.

Chapter Three: Childhood & Sexuality

THE SEXUAL SIN OF KING DAVID

We see an example of this in 2 Samuel 11:1-5.[1] It was a beautiful spring morning, and King David decided to walk around on the roof of the palace. This gave him a bird's eye view of the homes around him. While scanning the vicinity he saw a woman bathing; she was purifying herself from her monthly menstrual cycle. King David was drawn in by her beauty (Lust), so he inquired of her. His guards told him that she was Bathsheba, the wife of Uriah the Hittite. The fact that she was another man's wife did not faze him. This was King David's version of looking at porn, and he liked what he saw and wanted her delivered to his bed immediately.

The guards obeyed his commands by bringing the woman to his bed, where he forced himself on her. Satisfying his desires before dismissing her by sending her away once he was done. Weeks later, she sent word to him by messenger that she was pregnant, the news jolted him back to his senses. He then devised a scheme to cover up his mess. Her husband was a soldier in the King's army. At first, he was gracious to the man by ordering him to go home and spend time with his wife after he returned from war, but Uriah refused. His allegiance was to Israel and the King, so he slept at the palace entrance. When the guards told the King that Uriah did not go home, he sent a letter to the captain of the army telling him to put Uriah on the front line of battle when they returned to war.

The captain obeyed, and as a result, Uriah was killed. King David then married Bathsheba to cover up his sins. King David had no idea the chain of events he set in motion the day he committed adultery with this woman. If anyone in your bloodline engaged in sexual encounters with a woman during a menstrual cycle, this created a blood covenant of defilement with the kingdom of darkness.

Sexual Fantasy & The Christian Mind

Perverse acts such as this give the enemy the legal right to afflict generations of women with different uterine illnesses like fibroids, ovarian cancer, multiple miscarriages, infertility, and other female issues. To close this portal, you must repent on behalf of those who commit the sin and ask God to remove the sword of defilement from your bloodline. The notion of repenting on behalf of people you do not know is wild, especially ones who acted foolishly. You can either close the portal that the dummies unlocked or leave it open, cross your fingers, and pray that nothing bad happens to your children or future generations. In 2 Samuel 12:7-11, God uses the prophet Nathan to explain to King David the ramifications of his actions.

Verse 10 reads, *"Now, therefore,* **the sword** *will never depart from your house because you despised me and took the wife of Uriah the Hittite to be your own."*[1]

God was not pleased with David's behavior because he errored in his ways, just like some of your forefathers who sinned in the sight of God to appease their flesh while giving no thought to the impact their actions would have on future generations. Although God forgave King David because he quickly repented, the generational curse remained in his bloodline. The baby was stillborn, and in 2 Samuel 13:1-15,[1] King David's son Amnon fell in love with his sister because of her beauty (generational lust). Instead of asking his father for her hand in marriage, he concocted a devious plan with his cousin to lure her to his room by pretending to be sick.

Once she arrived with the meal she prepared for him, he overpowered her and raped her in the same manner his father raped Bathsheba. Verse 15 says, Then Amnon hated her with intense hatred. He hated her more than he had loved her. Amnon said to her, "Get up and get out!"[1] He threw her outside in the middle of the night. How many times have some of you experienced this? You met a person who began lusting after you? You then had a sexual exchange with them, and shortly after, they blocked you, ghosted you, or started playing games.

Chapter Three: Childhood & Sexuality

This is because the sword of defilement is dwelling in your bloodline; you are a Christian man or woman of God, so operating in the spirit of lust is a no, no. Both King David and Amnon allowed sexual fantasies to get the better of them. King David saw Bathsheba and began fantasizing about her beauty, maybe he thought about how soft her lips would feel when pressed against his. Years later, his son Amnon fell victim to the generational curse of sexual perversion that King David set in motion. Two years later, Tamar's brother Absalom devised a plan to kill his brother Amnon, the same way his father plotted against Uriah (Bathsheba's husband).

Absalom ordered his men telling them, "Listen! When Amnon is in high spirits from drinking wine, and I tell you, 'Strike Amnon down,' then kill him. Don't be afraid. Haven't I given you this order? Be strong and brave." Thus, Absalom's men did to Amnon what Absalom had ordered. Then, all the king's sons got up, mounted their mules, and fled." This is the aftermath of the enemy using his legal right obtained through adulterous acts to destroy a family. King David now had one son who was dead, a daughter who wished she was dead because she had been sentenced to a life of shame and loneliness, and another son on the run who later made attempts to wage war against his father's kingdom until finally he was destroyed by his anger.

The sword signifies authority, and when King David raped Bathsheba, he opened a demonic portal that gave the kingdom of darkness full authority to claim his bloodline. Contrary to popular belief Bathsheba did not sign up to be King David's side chic, she was carried to the palace against her will and thrown in his bed. The reason why she would not have agreed to be with the King is because they were still living under the Levitical law.

"If a man commits adultery with another man's wife—with the wife of his neighbor—both the adulterer and the adulteress must be put to death" (Leviticus 20:10).[1]

Chapter Three: Childhood & Sexuality

She was aware that if her husband discovered her infidelity, he would have sentenced her to death. King David's sexual misconduct was passed to his son who violated his sister and lost his life before he could make things right. He was not as remorseful as his father for his sinful act. It is the same as your ancestors who died not having a chance to undo their wrongs. Now, the responsibility of closing this portal falls on you. You will need to repent on their behalf as stated in Lamentations 5:7, *"Our fathers have sinned, and are not; and we have borne their iniquities."*

CHAPTER FOUR
MASTURBATION: THE POWER OF A TOUCH
Is Masturbation a sin?

Sexual Fantasy is the gateway the enemy uses to open the door of masturbation in your life, which in turn opens the portal of sexual perversion and the Marine Kingdom. This underwater world is ruled by the queen of the coast and is filled with seductive and mind-controlling spirits.[2] Levithan is a member of this kingdom (Isaiah 2:1, Job 41:1-34, Psalms. 74:13-14, Psalms 104:26, Revelation 20:2).[1] These demons are known as "water spirits" or "marine spirits." The devil controls three kingdoms: air, land, and sea. Ephesians 6:12 reads, *"For we wrestle not against flesh and blood, but against principalities, against powers, against the rulers of the darkness of this world, against spiritual wickedness in high places."*[1]

Ephesians 2:2 reads, *in which you used to live when you followed the ways of this world and of the ruler of the kingdom of the air, the spirit who is now at work in those who are disobedient.* Witches and warlocks employ the power of the air to astral travel, which is commonly referred to as astral projection. This technique allows them to enter your dreams and establish a profound connection with you, rendering it difficult for you to resist their influence when you encounter them in person.

Sexual Fantasy & The Christian Mind

Ezekiel 13:18 reads, *"Thus says the Lord GOD: Woe to the women who sew magic bands upon all wrists and make veils for the heads of persons of every stature, in the hunt for souls! Will you hunt down souls belonging to my people and keep your own souls alive."*[1]

The way to stop them from entering your dream at night is to ask God to cut their silver cord and break their golden bowl, as mentioned in Ecclesiastes 12:6. *"Before the silver cord is snapped, or the golden bowl is broken, or the pitcher is shattered at the fountain, or the wheel broken at the cistern."*[1] The activities of these spirits increase at night and with water. This is why the rain and the beaches are seen as romantic settings for making love. These spirits are assigned to regions (land) and can shapeshift to take on human form when on land, their agenda is to control the minds of men and women, getting them to commit lewd sexual acts on themselves and with young children.[5]

2 Corinthians 11:14 reads, *"And no wonder! For Satan himself transforms himself into an angel of light."*[1]

The effects of these spirits are lust and perversion. It is easy for them to possess humans. Our bodies are made of seventy percent water. They also have access to our dreams and can control our minds. A baby lives in water for nine months without drowning, and when a woman goes into labor, she says, "My water just broke." These spirits are responsible for infertility, and miscarriages. Leviathan, the sea creature of pride, is the strongest of these demons. Once he gets in, he remains hidden by wrapping himself around a person's spine. His strength is in the person's back and shoulders. When a person is filled with pride, the first thing they do is square their back and straighten their shoulders.

Chapter Four: Masturbation: The Power of A Touch

Once this demon gets in a person, he uses his scales from his back, which are called shield demons, to build strongholds in the person's life. Each demon is responsible for a stronghold; he then uses these strongholds to build a fortress around himself. With this type of covering, he can live in a person for years and go undetected. If the person tries to get delivered, he will give up a few of his shield demons but not himself,[3] for a person to get delivered from the spirit of Leviathan. They must find out how many shield demons he has protecting him. Once he tells you their names, they must be cast out individually.

When they are all gone, then he can be cast out. Disclaimer: please do not attempt to perform deliverance on yourself, instead, seek the help of your spiritual leaders. So, what does this spirit have to do with sexual fantasies? He will use pride to stop you from getting delivered. This spirit also causes baldness in women. (Isaiah 3:16-17),[1] Hair weaves, wigs, and hair extensions are sacrificed to the Marine Kingdom. The appearance of long hair is more alluring and seductive to men. Most men lust after women with long hair, whether it is real or fake. The next spirit in this kingdom that keeps you stuck in a cycle of sexual perversion is the mermaid spirit.[3]

This enticing spirit manifests itself in the form of the ideal woman or man of your preference, captivating you with every aspect of their being. This spirit utilizes the body of the person it possesses to lure married individuals into committing adultery. Once the deed is done, they gain a legal right to attack your finances by messing with your money.

Proverbs 6:32 reads, *"But a man who commits adultery has no sense; whoever does so destroys himself."*[1]

Proverbs 5:3-10 also reads,

"For the lips of the adulterous woman drip honey, and her speech is smoother than oil. But in the end, she is bitter as gall, sharp as a double-edged sword. Her feet go down to death; her steps lead straight to the grave. She gives no thought to the way of life; her paths wander aimlessly, but she does not know it. Now then, my sons, listen to me; do not turn aside from what I say. Keep to a path far from her, do not go near the door of her house, Lest you lose your honor to others and your dignity to one who is cruel, Lest strangers feast on your __wealth__ and your toil enrich the house of another." [1]

Hurt, deep pain, unforgiveness, masturbation, and sexual traumas give the Marine Kingdom a right to work in your life. Once a person becomes involved with sexual sins, this kingdom assigns you a spirit spouse who will mature with you through life.[5] Depending on what age this occurs, this spirit may lay dormant until you reach puberty, the hormonal changes will heighten your sexual desire. As a result of this new development, most teens begin masturbating and consuming porn. The word masturbation means stimulation of the genitals with the hand for sexual pleasure.[4]

This act satisfies the flesh, not God. John 3:6 reads, *"Flesh gives birth to flesh, but spirit gives birth to spirit."*[1] Committing sins of the flesh only takes you further away from God and deeper down the rabbit hole. God showed us in his word that he has all authority over the Marine Kingdom. Mark 4:39 reads *"And he awoke and rebuked the wind and said to the **sea**, "Peace! Be still!" And the wind ceased, and there was a great calm".*[1] In this verse, he speaks directly to the sea because he knows who is behind the raging storm. In Matthew 14:24-31,[1] the text says that Jesus walked on the sea, and the Marine Kingdom came subject under his feet. Verse 28 says Peter asked him to bid him to come unto him, but as he was walking to Jesus, he became afraid and started sinking, but while going under, he cried, "Lord, save me."[1]

Chapter Four: Masturbation: The Power of A Touch

Verse 31 says that Jesus immediately stretched out his hand and grabbed him. When you are drowning in sexual sin, God is waiting to hear those three words from you: "Lord, save me!"

Revelation 21:1 states, *"And I saw a new heaven and a new earth: for the first heaven and the first earth were passed away, and there was no more sea."*[1]

This scripture makes it clear that one day God will destroy and do away with the Marine Kingdom. After fasting for forty days and forty nights, the spirit led Jesus into the wilderness, where he encountered the devil, who took him to a high mountain in verse 8. In his weakened state, he overcame the devil, giving us control over the air (Matt. 4.8-11).[1] While on earth, Jesus cast out demons throughout his ministry and set the captive free. He is showing us that we have the power to overcome the devil on land, and he has given us the ability to do a more excellent work on the earth.

Psalms 34:15-20 reads, *"The eyes of the LORD are toward the righteous and his ears toward their cry. The face of the LORD is against those who do evil, to cut off the memory of them from the earth. When the righteous cry for help, the LORD delivers them out of all their troubles."*[1]

You are not waiting on God to move on your behalf, he is waiting on you to stop living in guilt and shame. God gave you dominion over the earth and everything in it to subdue it and put it under your feet. This includes the kingdom of sexual perversion. Now, it is time to answer the question that lingers in the minds of many Christian believers. Is masturbation a sin? After all the sex organs between your legs belong to you, God gave them to you. So, why would he have a problem with you touching them? It is not your fault they contain so many nerve endings that when touched in the right spot, it takes you to a state of ultimate climax.

Sexual Fantasy & The Christian Mind

Romans 8:8 tells us, "Those in the realm of the flesh cannot please God. "It is hard to focus on pleasing God when you are up late at night, spread eagle with your hand deep in the cookie jar—or sitting at the edge of your bed with only your socks on, treating your body part like a joystick to the newest video game. Ministry work becomes the least of your concerns as your eyes roll back in your head, and you are on the brink of transcending into a realm of total sexual bliss. It is at this very moment that you think to yourself, if masturbating is wrong, you do not want to be right. Although you initially wrestled with the thought of whether or not to masturbate, ultimately, you gave in.

This concession occurred because the enemy turned up the pressure by bombarding your mind with intense sexual imagery. He shot his fiery darts at your mind, and you failed to execute. 2 Corinthians 10:5-6, which reads, *"casting down imaginations, and every high thing that exalted itself against the knowledge of God and bringing into captivity every thought to the obedience of Christ, and having in a readiness to revenge all disobedience when your obedience is fulfilled."*[1]

Your failure to submit yourself to God and resist the devil so that he will flee from you (James 4:7)[1] gave him the opening he needed to bring your mind under sexual captivity. He broke down your spiritual defenses and got you to do exactly what he wanted. Afterward, you roll over and drift off to sleep, unaware of the magnitude of darkness you have unwittingly unleashed in your life and your home. God created the earth realm for humanity. In order for angels and demons to enter this realm, portals must be opened, granting them access. Each time you pray, you open heavenly dimensions that lead you to the throne room. Conversely, when you commit sexual sin via masturbation, or using sex toys, you open portals that lead to the kingdom of darkness.

Chapter Four: Masturbation: The Power of A Touch

Isaiah 45:12 reads, *"I am the one who made the earth and created people to live on it. With my hands, I stretched out the heavens. All the stars are at my command."*[1]

The devil and his demons can only operate in your life if they possess a legitimate authority to do so. Each time he releases a thought or command in your mind, and you obey him, he pulls you closer by increasing your appetite for sin. You begin craving and wanting more. Instead of masturbating only at night now, you find yourself committing the act at work, in your car, or at events. The need to masturbate now becomes an addiction, and you no longer have control over the urge, even when you do not feel like touching yourself, there is a demonic voice in your head bullying you. Telling you to "DO IT OR ELSE!." Masturbation is indeed sinful in God's sight.

SPIRIT SPOUSE

So, what comes next? The portal that you opened to the realm of darkness during masturbation assigned a spirit spouse to your life, and until you are delivered and set free, you are married to this demon. This is the reason why many of you remain single, or for those who are married, it contributes to trials within your marriage pushing you towards the brink of divorce. As these spirits assert their influence over you in the supernatural realm, they leave you emotionally unavailable to your spouse or potential spouse in the natural realm. Here are general signs that you can use to determine if you are married to a spirit spouse.[5]

- **Strange Dreams or Visions:**
  You might interpret dreams as messages from a spirit spouse. For instance, if you dream of having sex with a person or getting married to someone whose face you did not see or do not recognize, it could be perceived as communication from a spirit spouse.

- **Relationship Issues:**
  You consistently face stumbling blocks in your romantic relationships; it might be interpreted as interference from a spirit spouse. The difficulties you face in maintaining human relationships might be attributed to a spiritual connection with a spirit spouse. An individual you are dating breaks up with you without being able to give you a valid reason why.

- **Unexplained Illness or Misfortune:**
  Unexplained illnesses or misfortunes are often attributed to the influence of a spirit spouse. Conditions such as chronic and recurring diseases that are resistant and unresponsive to treatment may be seen as manifestations of spiritual interference. These could be ailments for which you have fervently prayed for healing but experienced no relief. As long as your spirit spouse maintains a legal foothold in your life, they will obstruct your healing and exacerbate your suffering. Once they engage in intimate relations with you, their goal is to ensnare your soul and drain your vitality.

  As John 10:10 states, *"The thief comes only to steal and kill and destroy; I have come that they may have life and have it to the fullest."*[1]

- **Unusual Behavior or Personality Changes:**
  A spirit spouse can cause abrupt changes in behavior or personality.

Chapter Four: Masturbation: The Power of A Touch

You might notice mood swings, feelings of sadness or depression, or an unexpected urge to alter your appearance, moving from conservative to revealing attire. You may also adjust your diet to include foods that are considered to be aphrodisiacs, which enhances your sex drive.

- **Feelings of Possession:**
  You may describe sensations of possession or external influence, attributing them to a spirit spouse. During the night, you may feel a deep urge to engage in sexual sin, starting with masturbation and escalating to a craving for physical intimacy with another person.

- **Challenges Socializing:**
  Getting out of the house to socialize with others is hard for you. While you eagerly make plans to meet up with family and friends, when the day of the event arrives, you find yourself coming up with excuses to avoid attending.

- **Personal Intuition or Guidance:**
  Some individuals assert having a strong intuition or inner guidance system that signals the presence of a spirit spouse, often sensing the feeling of a wedding ring on their left ring finger. Others may even comment that they assumed you were already married because you appeared to be taken.

These are only a few signs you may experience when married to a spirit spouse. It is worth taking the time to do your research to look for more. Incubus and Succubus are the two spirits who enter a spiritual marriage with you. Incubus is a demon who appears in male form to have sex with a woman while Succubus is the female version who has sex with males.[6]

Sexual Fantasy & The Christian Mind

They usually appear in your sleep, especially after you masturbate. Although you thought the sexual act you committed was with yourself, it was not. Your actions opened a portal in your life, giving them full access to you and everyone in your home. Your spirit spouse has a name, they will take on the name of your sex toys or one of your exes. If they allow you to marry a natural spouse once the honeymoon phase wears off, they will cause you to hate your spouse and will use you to say ugly things to them. This spirit operates from a place of jealousy and does not want to share you with another.[5]

People who are married have sex with each other, which makes it hard for your spirit spouse to have sex with you. This demon will cause you to mistreat your natural spouse by talking down to them and picking fights. This spirit wants you to emotionally abuse them, to get rid of them once the emotional trauma becomes too much for them to bear. When this happens, you will start feeling lonely and return to masturbating. A spirit spouse will make your natural spouse sick if they refuse to leave, they can also cause infertility, barrenness, and miscarriage in your marriage because they do not want you to have a baby with your actual spouse.

Often, if they are not able to kill the child in the womb, they will use the birth of the child to drive a wedge between you and your actual spouse. The goal of these spirits is to make your marriage sexless so you will divorce the person you are with and return to them. Many divorces happen because of these spirits. When you see families with multiple failed marriages, these spirits are moving through the bloodline. Having a relationship with a spirit spouse will make you lukewarm in God. This is also a spirit from the Marine Kingdom.[3]

Revelation 3:15-18 reads, *"I know your deeds, that you are neither cold nor hot. I wish you were either one or the other! So, because you are lukewarm hot nor cold-I am about to spit you out of my mouth."*[1] Engaging in masturbation or having sexual relations with a spirit spouse can lead to the sowing of corruptible seeds within you, that will manifest weeks later.

Chapter Four: Masturbation: The Power of A Touch

PLANTING A SEED

Sexual fantasy is a seed the enemy plants in your mind, given time to germinate it grows into full-on sexual misconduct. The idea of breaking free from these corruptible seeds and experiencing spiritual renewal is discussed in 1 Peter 1:23.[1] While some individuals may immediately recognize the effects of sexual sin, others may struggle at identify what is happening. A common aftermath of such actions is a profound sense of guilt or disbelief, weighing heavily on your conscience. This feeling may be described as a repulsive sense of regret, which leaves you thinking, "I can't believe I just touched myself."

You may even experience a strong urge to watch pornographic content afterward. These seeds are intentionally planted to remove any Godly seed the Holy Spirit sowed in you during worship or intimate moments in God's presence. The corruptible seed planted by your spirit spouse will cause you to have a spiritual miscarriage by hindering the growth of any divine seeds inside of you. This type of obstruction can disrupt the flow of God's anointing in your life. Leaving you feeling as though you have been abandoned and rejected by God. Being in this state can result in double-mindedness, making you feel unstable in every area of your life (James 1:8).[1]

It can also lead you to question the validity of God's written word and the promises he has spoken over your life through the word of knowledge. The negative influence of these doubts can stifle any potential for prosperity in your life, this explains why certain prophecies you received may not come to fruition. The devil's intention behind this is to disrupt your faith in God. When you believe that God has forsaken you, it can lead to feelings of hopelessness and despair. This loss of trust in God's promises will cast a shadow of despair over your mind, making everything seem bleak.

Chapter Four: Masturbation: The Power of A Touch

The adversary capitalizes on this vulnerability by infiltrating your mind with negative thoughts. The seeds of doubt that have been planted will compromise your defenses, leaving you in a state of spiritual weakness, making it difficult for you to concentrate or pray. This defenselessness opens you up to the influence of your spirit spouse. These entities will transition you from having sex with yourself to desiring physical intimacy with another person. There are spiritual laws that govern the earth realm, and the enemy cannot violate these laws, or he will deal with the consequences of his actions.

His objective is to engage you in sexual immortality to possess and control your mind, ultimately leading your soul to eternal torment in hell. As the effects of these spiritual encounters manifest, you may find yourself battling with self-loathing behaviors such as self-hatred, self-sabotage, low self-esteem, self-pity, and more. You may feel a strong urge to isolate yourself from others. This is the prep work Satan does before fully possessing you. There are steps to possession, this is because of the free will of humanity. You have to surrender your free will to the devil before he can take possession of your soul. He takes a part of your free will each time you commit sexual sin.

The steps to a person becoming demon-possessed **are sadness, depression, oppression**, and then **possession.**[7] Once you become possessed, you are now a slave to sin. This is where many Christians start hiding from their leaders, hanging with the wrong crowd, start missing church, having sex with multiple partners, experimenting with same-sex partners, having threesomes, anal sex, golden showers, whips, chains, bondage, experimenting with sex toys, and visiting sex dens.

Chapter Four: Masturbation: The Power of A Touch

MIND CONTROL SPIRITS

The act of using masturbation as a method of self-gratification or self-soothing pleasure is directly linked to the kingdom of darkness. Masturbation affects your commitment to God by blinding your spiritual eyes, dulling your spiritual ears, and closing your mouth so you cannot pray. This is known as the deaf, dumb, and blind spirit. It also opens the door to sexual immorality, and over time, this spirit will claim every member of your household. This act of sexual perversion will hinder your spiritual growth and lead you deeper into sin, making you a prisoner to your fleshly desires.

Godly sex was created for the married bed for spirit-to-spirit connection and communion with the person God has chosen for you to grow old with. This is the reason the enemy introduced you to masturbating at an early age so that he can connect you with a spirit spouse. There is no true fulfillment in masturbating. Once the action is complete, it leaves you feeling lonely, isolated, ashamed, and empty. The enemy uses masturbation to play tricks on your mind, making you feel as if you need to masturbate for physical release. However, with time, the practice of masturbating will create difficulties for you in your spiritual and natural life.

Your desire for self-pleasure is governed by the spirit of sexual perversion, which is from the Marine Kingdom. Masturbation releases mind-controlling spirits in your life (the squid and the octopus). Their tentacles grasp and control your mind. They create mental pressure (migraine headaches), confusion, mental torment, and memory loss. They also create brain fog, these spirits build a stronghold around your mind, making it hard for you to think clearly or hear from God.[3] Once this stronghold is in place, the enemy creates habits in your life so you can feed the strong man. This makes him grow and develop other addictions in your life that open more demonic portals.

Sexual Fantasy & The Christian Mind

These demons will control every aspect of your life, when you do not want to masturbate, they will force you into touching yourself. The Devil wants you to masturbate while watching porn so your brain can connect the imagery to your emotions. This will trigger within you the need to masturbate leaving you feeling helpless against his entrapment. He will also manipulate your thoughts, which leads to forgetfulness, out of frustration, you will begin using profanity to express yourself.

LAYING ON OF HANDS

Typically, when a person believes they are demon-possessed, the usual course of action is to head to the altar. Then the pastor steps in and lay hands to get them delivered, it is important to note that this deliverance process often results in the freedom of just one person. The kingdom of darkness mimics the kingdom of light. Satan cages your soul by convincing you to engage in sexual acts with multiple partners to increase your body count. The pastor laid his hands to set your soul free, and the devil uses your hands to bind it up again. This is called the power of a touch, and it is done through masturbation, adultery, or fornication—however, the effects of this touching are the opposite of spiritual deliverance.

Spiritual deliverance only frees one person at a time, but sexual corruption defiles many at one encounter through the exchange of soul ties. The bottom line is the devil hates God, and he hates you even more. He wants to stop you from advancing in the kingdom of light by filling you with his darkness. He was kicked out of heaven and rejected by God because of his misconduct (Isaiah 14:12-15),[1,] and now, he wants you to suffer the same fate. His goal is to pervert you and prostitute your spiritual gifts by getting you to use them for evil instead of good. He knows that God takes no pleasure in the death of the wicked (Ezekiel. 18:32),[1] although his fate is sealed in the lake of fire.

Chapter Four: Masturbation: The Power of A Touch

It still does not stop him from trying to take as many of God's people with him as possible. He may be out of options, but you are not. As long as you have breath in your body, you still have a chance to repent of your sins and receive reconciliation. Call on God out of a sincere heart, and he will answer you and set you free. Do not allow the enemy of your soul to win by taking you deeper into sin. Hell was not made for you, it was designed for the devil and his demons. Though you are broken, let Father put you back together again. Decide today that you no longer want to live in sin and shame. You are not the only person going through this. Jesus died for your sins; he is your safe place. He came that you may have life & have it more abundantly (John 10:10).[1]

WEIRD WARFARE

Weird warfare is when you find yourself doing something against your natural and spiritual morals and beliefs. So, what happened? How in the world did you get yourself into this mess? One minute you are in church serving God with all your heart, the next, you are in a hotel room screaming, "SPANK ME, DADDY! IT'S YOURS!" Or maybe you are a man who finds himself in the bed of a strange woman, asking her "WHAT'S MY NAME? YEAH! YOU LIKE THAT? I SAID DO-YOU-LIKE-THAT?" How did the sons and daughters of God get caught up in the sins of the flesh? Well, it is a tale as old as time, it is just filled with more beast than beauty.

You were drawn away and enticed by your own lust (James 1:4-16).[1] And lust, after it was conceived, produced sin which brought forth a spiritual death. You failed to protect your gates, and as the word says, whatsoever is done in the dark shall come to light (Luke 12:2-3).[1] **REPENT** of your sins today and get back in right standing with God, because tomorrow might be too late.

Sexual Fantasy & The Christian Mind

COVERING YOUR GATES

"And I say unto thee, that thou art Peter, and upon this rock I will build my church; and the gates of hell shall not prevail against it (Matthew 16:18)."[1] In this verse, Jesus uses the word "gates," in plural form meaning more than one. Dealing with sexual fantasies of the mind will open you up to many gates in the spirit realm. Leaving these gates open in your life allows the strong man to overpower you and keep you trapped. Each gate symbolizes a spiritual tie binding you to becoming a puppeteer fit for the devil's use.

Here are the gates that all believers should protect from the enemy.

Eye ……	What you see
Ear ……	What you listen to
Mouth …	What you speak
Nose ……	Things you smell
Heart …..	What/who you let in
Touch ….	Who you connect to
Feet ……	Places you travel

Proverbs 4:23-27 states, *"Guard your heart above all else, for it determines the course of your life. Avoid all perverse talk; stay away from corrupt speech. Look straight ahead and fix your eyes on what lies before you. Mark out a straight path for your feet; stay on the safe path. Don't get sidetracked; keep your feet from following evil."*[1] Let's look at these gates, starting with the Eye.

Chapter Four: Masturbation: The Power of A Touch

Matthew 6:22-24 reads, *"The eye is the lamp of the body. If your eyes are healthy, your whole body will be full of light. But if your eyes are unhealthy, your whole body will be full of darkness."*[1] As a Christian believer, you already know the prerequisite required to keep your eyes full of light. What caused your eyes to go dark?

Galatians 5:9-10 reads, *"A little leaven leavens the whole lump. I have confidence in you, in the Lord, that you will have no other mind; but he who troubles you shall bear his judgment, whoever he is."* [1]

As a modern-day Christian, you face a lot of visual imagery, many of which plant corruptible seeds in your mind while robbing you of spending time with God. Most Christians wake up in the morning grabbing their cell phones for a shot of dopamine instead of their Bibles to check for missed messages, phone calls, and alerts. This is called the blue light special, it is a trap set by the enemy of your soul. The distraction begins when you respond to a message or open a link sent from a friend. Next thing you know hours have passed and you are still looking at social media content, many of which are filled with sexual imagery and innuendos. Sexual fantasies sparked your curiosity, which led to an addiction to porn; The enemy uses sexual fantasies linked to the media as daily tools to keep you disconnected from fellowship with God.

Sexual Fantasy & The Christian Mind

THE EYE

"The eyes are the window to your soul"(Matt. 6.22-24).[1]

Entertainment has changed over the years. Comedy shows have lost their innocence, the nightly news is filled with negativity, and most major networks have thrown the rule book out the window. They are baring it all, leaving nothing to the imagination. Watching shows like "Power," Sista's, "All the Queen's Men," and "Baller" will leave you hot and horny before the first commercial. Media has the power to model, alter, change, and control your mind's perception of reality with imagery. Most of the shows you watch tell a false narrative; they only show you the actions but never the consequences. Producers cast good-looking actors and actresses whose physical appearance feeds into your sexual desires.

Ephesians 6:12 reads, *"We are not wrestling against flesh & blood but against the principalities of the air, rulers of darkness."*[1]

Who is influencing producers to create the shows you are currently watching? The networks are commonly referred to as airwaves, and the devil is known as the prince of the air (Ephesians 2:2). The content broadcasted on these networks has a significant impact on your mental well-being. Consuming inappropriate programs and music can gradually lead to feelings of inadequacy, isolation, and depression. Your mind serves as the battleground where the enemy launches attacks against you. Indulging in explicit content for extended periods grants the enemy direct access to your soul. For instance, viewing pornography.

Chapter Four: Masturbation: The Power of A Touch

Many may wrestle with the question, "Is looking at porn a sin?" 1 Thessalonians 4:3 encourages us to abstain from sexual immorality,[1] Psalm 119:37 reads, *"Turn my eyes from looking at worthless things, and give me life in your ways.*[1] Looking at porn is a sin that soils the eyes and corrupts the soul, which Makes it hard for you to see a pure God through perverted eyes. Consequently, your soul records and stores information the enemy can later manipulate to control your emotions. It is essential to understand that what you input determines what you output therefore, consuming negative content will result in negativity.

The enemy uses soul ties to keep you ensnared. While many Christians associate soul ties solely with sexual encounters, there are other forms as well. "Soul ties" refer to deep emotional or spiritual connections between individuals, although the concept may vary across different belief systems.[8] The idea of soul ties is often rooted in the notion that individuals can become deeply connected on a spiritual or emotional level. These connections can have various effects on their lives and relationships.

Here are a few interpretations or types of soul ties that you may be unaware of.

Positive Soul Ties:

- **Friendship Ties:** Deep, meaningful connections formed through friendship.

- **Family Ties:** Bonds between family members, such as parent-child or sibling relationships.

- **Marriage Ties:** The connection formed between spouses in a committed, loving marriage.

Sexual Fantasy & The Christian Mind

Negative Soul Ties:

- o **Toxic Relationships:** Unhealthy connections that can be emotionally, spiritually damaging, and draining.

- o **Unhealthy Attachments:** Obsessive or controlling connections that hinder spiritual and personal growth.

- o **Destructive Bonds:** Connections formed through negative experiences or trauma.

- o **Emotional Soul Tie:**
  You are immediately drawn to this person, regardless of how badly they treat you. Breaking free from them seems impossible; your soul craves their presence and their touch, and being apart makes you sick. This kind of soul tie often involves some form of divination. A porn addiction can also be linked to this type of soul tie.

Sexual Soul Ties:

- o **Sexual Connections:** The idea that sexual relationships create a deep spiritual or emotional bond.

- o **Premarital or Casual Sex Ties:** Engaging in sexual activity outside of marriage can create negative soul ties.

- o **Sex Toys:** It is formed from the molding of a real penis causing you to form a soul tie with the person it belongs to. The phrase "God broke the mold when he made you" just took on a whole new meaning.

Chapter Four: Masturbation: The Power of A Touch

Your soul houses your emotions and your intellect; God designed your soul to process the information seen by your eyes. If you are a Christian who spends more time on worldly pursuits than in God's presence, you leave yourself vulnerable to darkness overwhelming your soul. Once this occurs, it becomes easier for the enemy to influence your mind. You may hear his voice commanding you to indulge in porn, watch R-rated movies, or listen to music with explicit lyrics and look at entertainment with pornographic content that will take over your mind and dominate your thoughts. So, I ask you again. What are you watching, and how is it impacting your walk with God?

THE EAR

What type of music are you listening to? What type of conversation are you entertaining? As a Christian, you are responsible for keeping the lines of communication open between yourself and the Holy Spirit. Sexual sin is a communication blocker because it stops you from hearing God. If you are unable to hear from the father, this will cause you to miss divine appointments. The enemy will also use this opportunity to activate a deaf, dumb, and blind spirit in your life. Your involvement with sexual perversion gives him the legal right to block your visions, dreams, and downloads from the Lord. When you dream, upon waking up, you will not remember the details of your dream.

You are like a cell phone filled with capabilities but limited by a low signal. You are experiencing divine blockers when you are out of sync with the Holy Spirit, being in this state creates a glass ceiling in your life to keep your prayers earthbound. The ear is directly connected to your brain. Speech, noise, and sound are processed through brain waves. So, what you hear or listen to affects your thought pattern.

Sexual Fantasy & The Christian Mind

For instance, if you are addicted to watching porn, once you hear the sexual groanings of men or women, you will experience immediate arousal. When you listen to music with explicit lyrics, you will want to act out the words played in the song. Before Jesus departed from the earth, he said, "If I do not go, the comforter will not come." He referred to the Holy Spirit as our comforter and guide. His assignment is to lead and guide the believer into all truth. The Holy Spirit wants to communicate with you daily, but if you are committing acts of sexual perversion, your sin will be like a wall between you and God.

Isaiah 59:2 reads, *"But your iniquities have separated you from your God; And your sins have hidden His face from you, So that He will not hear. For your hands are defiled with blood, And your fingers with iniquity; Your lips have spoken lies, Your tongue has muttered perversity."*[1]

THE MOUTH

Be careful of what you say when upset, especially when you grow tired of life's circumstances. *"Life and death are in the power of the tongue"* (Prov. 18.21).[1] *"You shall have whatever you say"* (Mark 11.23).[1] God used his words to form the world, and you have the same ability on the inside of you. It is called the God factor, the words you spoke yesterday created your world today, and the words you speak today will form your world tomorrow. Your words shape your world, so what do you want your world to look like years from now? Choose your words wisely to avoid having any regrets. Your mouth was made to worship God.

"My mouth is filled with your praise, declaring your splendor all day" (Psalm. 71:8).[1] You can maintain focus by watching your mouth. Controlling your speech is critical in this next phase of your life. Be mindful of what you say and how it is being said. Proverbs 21:23 reads, *"Those who guard their mouths, and their tongues keep themselves from calamity."*[1]

Chapter Four: Masturbation: The Power of A Touch

The wrong words spoken against yourself can be destructive to your destiny. If you are operating under mind-controlling spirits, the negative internal dialogue taking place in your head is not your own. You are being told what to think; you are not in your right mind. Demon possession impairs your mind's ability to think Godly thoughts; it blocks them from getting in. Ephesians 4:29 reads, *"Do not let any unwholesome talk come out of your mouths, but only what helps build others up according to their needs, that it may benefit those who listen."*[1]

THE NOSE

Imagine sitting in your living room when you hear music from the television. You stop what you are doing and glance up, only to see another one of those senseless perfume ads playing. It features a handsome, shirtless man wearing dark-washed jeans, running towards the edge of a cliff to leap into the ocean after spraying on cologne. Shortly after, it is the woman's turn; she is running barefoot towards the sea in an elegant, expensive evening gown, with a stern expression on her face. As she plunges into the water, the second camera captures her underwater. At the same time, a soft, seductive voice reveals the perfume's name.

For someone viewing this commercial with a carnal mindset, their reaction might be, "Wow, I need that perfume." However, God's children should refrain from such simplistic thinking. The commercial conveyed all the necessary information. The fragrance is seductive and alluring, designed to connect you with sexual spirits from the Marine Kingdom. It is illogical for someone to purchase expensive perfume, apply it, and then dive into the ocean. The commercial planted a dark seed of seduction in your mind. Many men and women have fallen prey to the alluring fragrance they smelled on someone else in passing. Your nose can lead you into temptation (Matthew 6:11-13).[1]

When fasting, the sensors in your nose become heightened. Your nose serves as a source of discernment, distinguishing between what is rotten and what is good.

The Heart

God asked a question in his word. *"If your heart convicts you, am I not greater than your heart?"* (1 John 3.20-24).[1] Also, in the Old Testament, God said he would remove a heart of stone out of you and replace it with a heart of flesh (Ezekiel. 36:26).[1] Once you become entangled with sexual sin, a callus begins to grow around your heart, which creates a hardening. The more this growth progresses, the harder it gets for God to prick your heart so his word can flow in you. Disappointment rooted in a negative inner dialogue will leave you in a state of hopelessness.

1 Corinthians 6:18 reads, *"Flee from sexual immorality. All other sins a person commits are outside the body, but whoever sins sexually, sins against their own body. Do you not know that your bodies are temples of the Holy Spirit, who is in you, whom you have received from God?"*[1]
Committing sexual sin is a matter of the heart, the seed of perversion is planted in your mind, but it takes root in your heart. Allowing the Holy Spirit to live on the inside of you is a matter of the heart because you have to open up your heart and let him in.

The Hands

When dealing with the spirit of sexual perversion, it is crucial to exercise caution regarding physical contact with others. Be mindful of who you touch and who you permit to touch you. There is a law of transference whereby spirits can move from one individual to another through touch. This transfer is not confined to specific settings, it can occur at church, massage parlors, doctors' offices, hair salons, and during sexual acts.

Chapter Four: Masturbation: The Power of A Touch

When you closely interact with someone who possesses a stronger demonic spirit than the presence of your own, there is a risk of those spirits transferring over to you. Consequently, this transfer will leave you susceptible to being influenced by the spirits they entertain. If you are unfamiliar with a person, it is advisable to refrain from physical contact and to prevent them from touching you or anything that belongs to you. This precaution helps guard against the inadvertent transfer of demonic spirits. Engaging in one-night stands, random hookups with strangers, or cheating on your spouse with someone new (or old) will increase your chances of becoming a recipient of this law. The hand represents outreach, power, and authority.

THE FEET

"And how shall they preach unless they are sent? As it is written: "How beautiful are the feet of those who preach the gospel of peace, who bring glad tidings of good things!" (Romans 10:15). [1] God designed your feet to tread on serpents and scorpions, and nothing shall by any means hurt you. Why are you using your blessed feet to do the will of the enemy instead of the work of God? Many of you refuse to travel for ministry but will pack your bags for a trip to the beach in a heartbeat to indulge in what you call guilt-free sex, or so you think. No matter where you commit sexual sin, God sees you.

Psalms 139:7-10 reads, *"If I ascend into heaven, you are there; If I make my bed in hell, behold, you are there. If I take the wings of the morning, and dwell in the uttermost parts of the sea, even there Your hand shall lead me, and your right hand shall hold me."* [1]

Sexual Fantasy & The Christian Mind

It is time for you to refrain from using your feet to travel to have sex with strangers, meeting them in their homes, hotels, rooftops, or the back seat of a car. The feet represent humility, servitude, and guidance, it can also be seen as a symbol of enlightenment.[1] Gates has profound symbolic significance, representing entry points, authority, and communal spaces.[1] In the context of spiritual warfare within Christianity, gates hold a symbolic value as entry points for spiritual attack. Covering the gates under the blood of Jesus acknowledges the power of Jesus' death on the cross to cleanse you of your sins and protect you from demonic influences.

Psalm 121:7-8 reads, *"The Lord will keep you from all harm—he will watch over your life; the Lord will watch over your coming and going both now and always."*[1]

Through prayer, God has given you the power to make a clean getaway from the enemy by seeking divine intervention and protection over your home, lives, and loved ones. The act of covering entrances in worship is an expression of dependence on God's guidance and safeguarding. Covering the gates under the blood of Jesus and invoking guardian angels are spiritual practices you should practice while seeking your deliverance. It reflects a deep trust in the redemptive power of Jesus' sacrifice and his protective role in your life. This practice is not a formula for warding off all challenges but serves as a symbolic expression of faith and dependence on God's guidance and protection.

Believers engaging in sexual fantasies are encouraged to protect their gates by creating an environment where the presence of God is welcomed, and evil forces find no entrance. As you navigate this spiritual rebirthing, embracing these practices will contribute to your holistic spiritual protection and well-being.

Chapter Four: Masturbation: The Power of A Touch

BREAKING FREE

Now that you understand how soul ties are formed, how can you break free from them? Breaking a soul tie takes work; you must be consistent and intentional. *Matthew 17:20-21 reads, "This kind comes by prayer and fasting."*[1] If you have anything tangible in your home binding you to a soul tie, gifts, pictures, sex toys, or clothing, get rid of it. Delete the app, website, or movie channel if the soul tie is linked to entertainment. Be sure to unsubscribe from all monthly subscriptions. Next, you will need to contact your leaders or a Godly mentor who is stronger than you to confess your sins and ask them to help you get delivered by the power and anointing of God.

You will need to renounce all connections to the realm of darkness; you will also need to close all portals that you opened knowingly and unknowingly. If the soul tie involves a sexual partner or a close confidant, you will need to call out their first and last name and send their spirit back to them. After all this is done, you will need to fast and pray to fill the void in you with God's light. So, when the enemy returns, he will only see the light of God and not an old, familiar place filled with void.

Matthew 12:43-45 reads, *"When the unclean spirit is gone out of a man, he walketh through dry places, seeking rest, and findeth none Then he saith, I will return into my house from whence I came out. When he comes, he findeth it empty, swept, and garnished Then goeth he, and taketh with himself seven other spirits more wicked than himself, and they enter in and dwell there: and the last state of that man is worse than the first. Even so, shall it be also unto this wicked generation."*

A BYPRODUCT OF SEXUAL FANTASY

Lust is often considered a byproduct of sexual fantasy as it involves imagining or visualizing different sexual scenarios, triggering feelings of desire and arousal. Here is the reason why lust often emerges because of sexual fantasies.

- **Stimulation of Desires:** Sexual fantasies are intentionally designed to stimulate and enhance sexual desires. When we engage in these fantasies, our minds conjure up scenarios that align with our deepest desires and interests, intensifying our longing and craving.

- **Escapism and Gratification:** Sexual fantasies can serve as an escape from reality. They allow individuals to experience pleasure and excitement in their imagination, even without engaging in sexual activities. This sense of gratification can lead to heightened lust as the mind seeks to fulfill those desires.

- **Focus on Sensual Pleasure:** Sexual fantasies often revolve around intense sensory experiences, focusing on physical sensations, pleasure, and arousal. This heightened focus on the sensory aspects of sex can contribute to an increased desire for those sensations in real life.

- **Amplification of Fantasized Scenarios:** Over time, repeated engagement with sexual fantasies can strengthen these scenarios in the mind. The more one indulges in these thoughts, the more the stories can become ingrained, further fueling feelings of lust associated with them.

Chapter Four: Masturbation: The Power of A Touch

- **Disconnection from Reality:** While sexual fantasies can provide temporary pleasure and excitement, they can also create a disconnect from the realities of real-life relationships and intimacy. This disconnect can intensify lust as the fantasies become divorced from human connections' emotional and relational aspects.

- **Lack of Boundaries:** In some cases, sexual fantasies may involve scenarios that lack boundaries or ethical considerations. This lack of restraint can contribute to unchecked feelings of lust, as you engage in mentally simulated situations that you would not pursue in real life.

The Damaging Effects of Lust
Sexual Fantasy + Lust = Sexual Immorality

A Spirit spouse will remain active in your life when you operate from a place of lust, they want you to have sexual cravings toward others. It starts with you lusting after your favorite singer or movie star. The carnal mind dismisses this as normal, but it is not. Once you begin to lust after a person, it is only a matter of time before you start having sex with them in your mind. Lust is regarded as a sin according to the teachings of the Bible (James 1:14-16).[1] It is seen as a manifestation of unfaithfulness and immorality that originates from worldly influences rather than from God. The Scriptures advise believers to be vigilant against succumbing to lustful desires (Matthew 5:28).[1]

1 John 2:16-17 reads,
"For everything in the world—the lust of the flesh, the lust of the eyes, and the pride of life—comes not from the Father but from the world."[1]

Mark-7:20-23 also reads,
"And then he added, 'It is what comes from inside that defiles you. For from within, out of a person's heart, come evil thoughts, sexual immorality, theft, murder, adultery, greed, wickedness, deceit, lustful desires, envy, slander, pride, and foolishness. All these vile things come from within; they are what defile you."[1]

GAINING CONTROL OVER LUST

Lust is a sensation that nearly all of us have encountered, and society consistently encourages it in various ways. Nonetheless, believers are encouraged to take active measures to counteract its influence over them and avoid lust at all costs. Even in instances when God reveals your potential spouse as you spend time getting to know each other, it is imperative to steer clear of lust. You may start to develop lustful feelings for this person based on the strong physical attraction. It may begin innocently; however, the more you think about them when you are apart, the more likely it is for your thoughts to become sexual. Getting married and being married is not the same thing. The following scripture on lust reads.

1 Thessalonians 4:3-5
"For this is the will of God, your sanctification: that you should <u>abstain</u> from sexual immorality; that each of you should know how to possess his own vessel in sanctification and honor, not in passion of lust, like the Gentiles who do not know God."[1]

Colossians 3:5
"So put to death the sinful, earthly things lurking within you. Have nothing to do with sexual immorality, impurity, lust, and evil desires. Don't be greedy, for a greedy person is an idolater, worshiping the things of this world.[1]

Chapter Four: Masturbation: The Power of A Touch

The damaging effects of lust in the life of a Christian when it comes to dealing with sexual fantasies are like walking a tightrope between faith and desire. Sometimes, that balance can feel elusive. Your mind feels like it is unraveling as you navigate the complexities and debunk the myths of understanding these thoughts. Developing a causal mindset towards the spirit of lust allows this sin to hide in the recesses of your mind, most Christians do not see lust as an area of concern. Instead, they say "everyone does it, so it's no big deal," but dealing with lust is a big deal.

Lust, if left unchecked, can muddy the waters of the Christian mind, making it difficult for you to be able to draw a clear line of demarcation between what is clean vs. unclean. Instead of looking at lust from a sensual point of view, let us put on our Christian lenses and examine what we mean by lust in the context of faith. Lust, in the biblical sense, is not just about sexual desire but an intense craving that goes beyond God's intended boundaries. It is an all-consuming longing that pulls you away from the righteousness of God's plan for your life. The scriptures provide a clear stance on the potential pitfalls of unchecked lust.

Matthew 5:28 reads, *"for instance, where Jesus addresses the matter of the heart: "But I tell you that anyone who looks at a woman lustfully has already committed adultery with her in his heart."*

This verse emphasizes the significance of outward actions and inner thoughts and desires. It underscores the idea that lust is not just a fleeting thought but a matter that strikes at the core of your integrity and commitment to God's commandments.

Sexual Fantasy & The Christian Mind

CHRISTIANITY AND SEXUAL PURITY

Christianity places a high value on sexual purity. The Bible emphasizes the sanctity of the marital relationship and cautions against engaging in sexual activities outside the bounds of marriage. For Christians, the damaging effects of lust are intertwined with the broader concept of sexual purity and the call to honor God with your body.

1 Corinthians 6:18 reads, *"Flee from sexual immorality. All other sins a person commits are outside the body, but whoever sins sexually sins against their own body."*[1]

This verse highlights the gravity of sexual sins and reinforces the call to resist the pull of lustful desires. The more you allow lust to intensify in your life, the more susceptible you will be to masturbating. It will be easier for you to touch yourself because you will imagine someone touching you instead of you touching yourself. This heightens the climax and lessens the guilt. This is particularly true on rainy nights and during cold weather. These are only a few aspects of the damaging effects of lust on the Christian believer. This release may have brought momentary joy to your body, but it leaves your mind in turmoil.

In the morning, when you awake to pray or enter into worship with God, your spirit feels heavy because the guilt of what you did the night before is still lingering over you. Each time you close your eyes to pray or lift your hands to worship, a voice from within condemns you, leaving you feeling fake and pretentious. If you have any church activity that week, it will cause you to hide from your leaders.

Chapter Four: Masturbation: The Power of A Touch

Hiding from God after committing sin is another generational curse you need to overcome. This behavior was passed down to you from Adam and Eve. Genesis 3:8 tells us, "The man and his wife hid themselves from the presence of God among the trees of the garden." Until this curse is broken, you will always hide from God in an attempt to cover your sins. The longer these thoughts torment your mind, the further you drift from God's presence. You desperately want to repent and get back in place, but you are overcome with regret thinking about all the times you made God a promise telling him it was the last time.

Now, here you are right back where you were before wallowing in your filth yet again. Lust can drive a wedge between an individual and their relationship with God. The guilt that often accompanies lustful thoughts can make you feel unworthy in God's eyes. This perceived separation can hinder your ability to approach God with an open heart filled with true intimacy which is essential to your faith. The conflict between your faith and your values can create a profound sense of guilt—the feeling of falling short of God's expectations of you can add another layer to your struggle.

This level of guilt will leave you believing you are fundamentally flawed or unworthy of God's love due to your thoughts and desires. This emotional weight can be overwhelming and may lead you to withdraw from your faith community, exacerbating the sense of isolation.

Addressing guilt and shame involves:
- Recognizing them as human emotions.
- Understanding their source.
- Seeking avenues for healing and forgiveness.

Sexual Fantasy & The Christian Mind

Christianity teaches that confession, repentance, and seeking God's mercy are vital steps in finding redemption from guilt and shame. Feeling distant from God can be a heavy burden, and the damaging effects of lust may amplify this sense of separation. Individuals must recognize that God's grace is boundless and that the doors toward redemption are always open.

In Matthew 18:21-35, *"Peter asked Jesus a question. He said, "Lord, how many times will my brother sin against me, and I forgive him and let it go? Up to seven times? Jesus answered him, I say to you no, not up to seven times, but seventy times seven."*[1]

Here is the good news after reading this verse, Jesus will never ask us to do things he has not exemplified for us to follow. You cannot remain in this place of guilt and pain. The Holy Spirit has given you enough information on the pages of this book to get to the root of why you do what you do. Now it is time to pull out your spiritual sword (The word of God) and chop the tree of masturbation down once and for all. It is time for you to walk in freedom.

Romans 8:1 reads, *"There is, therefore, no condemnation to them, which are in Christ Jesus, who walk not after the flesh but after the Spirit."*[1] The act of sexual sin only lasts for a short while, and then it is over. If you are a true believer, you are the bride of Christ, and it is time to rid yourself of all sexual impropriety.

Ephesians 5:26-27 reminds us, *"That He might present her to Himself a glorious church, not having spot or wrinkle or any such thing, but that she should be holy and without blemish."*[1]

Indulging in acts of self-touch and sexual sin creates spots, wrinkles, and blemishes on your spiritual garment. The King of Glory is looking for clean vessels to carry his anointing.

Chapter Four: Masturbation: The Power of A Touch

This is why he purified you from all sins and unrighteousness the day he saved you. We are living in the last and final days; Jesus is soon to crack the sky. You do not want to miss the rapture because when it occurs, you are busy fantasizing, looking at porn, masturbating, or immersed in sexual sin. **REPENT** of your sins and get your house in order before it's too late.

DISTORTED VIEW OF SEXUALITY

The damaging consequence of lust extends beyond your connection with God and with others. In the context of personal relationships, lust can strain the bonds of trust and intimacy within a marriage or partnership. For Christians, the call to honor the sanctity of marriage is central, and engaging in lustful thoughts or behaviors outside the marital covenant can be perceived as a breach of that commitment. The potential erosion of trust and emotional intimacy can lead to challenges in communication and connection within the relationship. Transparent conversation and seeking counseling, whether from pastoral or professional sources, can be vital in addressing the impact of lust on personal relationships.

Recognizing the need for healing and taking proactive steps to rebuild trust can contribute to restoring healthy relationships. Lust can contribute to a skewed opinion of sexuality within the Christian framework. The emphasis on sexual purity can sometimes lead to viewing sex as inherently sinful or taboo outside the confines of marriage. This perspective can hinder a healthy understanding of God's gift of sexuality within the framework of marriage. Addressing a distorted view of sexuality involves engaging in studying your word and having open and honest conversations with other believers, or the faith-based community. Creating a safe space for dialogue about the intersection of faith and sexuality can foster a more balanced understanding of God's design for human sexuality.

Chapter Four: Masturbation: The Power of A Touch

HINDRANCE TO YOUR SPIRITUAL GROWTH

A continuous pursuit of spiritual growth and maturity marks the plight of a Christian. Lust can become a stumbling block on this path, diverting focus and energy from spiritual actions. When desires become all-consuming, the time and energy devoted to prayer, studying scripture, and serving others may be compromised. The process of spiritual growth requires intentional effort, and addressing the destructive effects of lust involves redirecting focus toward deepening your relationship with God to mitigate the detrimental effects of lust. Recognizing the impact of lustful thoughts, confessing them in prayer, and genuinely repenting are foundational steps toward finding forgiveness and moving forward in your spiritual growth.
Psalm 51:10 reads, *"Create in me a pure heart, O God, and renew a steadfast spirit within me."*[1]

This psalm for renewal and purity reflects the Christian belief in the transformative power of God's grace. Prayer is a powerful tool in navigating the challenges posed by lust. Engaging in regular prayer, seeking guidance, and surrendering your struggles to God can foster a sense of connection and reliance on divine strength. In addition to prayer, participating in spiritual disciplines such as fasting, meditation, stirring up the gifts on the inside of you, and studying scripture can contribute to a deeper understanding of your faith and provide the strength needed to overcome the damaging repercussions of lust. The Christian walk is not meant to be walked alone. Establishing relationships with fellow believers who share similar struggles creates a network of encouragement, understanding, and mutual support.

James 5:16 reads, *"Confess your faults one to another, and pray one for another, that ye may be healed. The effectual fervent prayer of a righteous man availeth much."*

CHAPTER FIVE
GODLY DATING
Should a Christian date?

In this chapter, we aim to address the elephant in the room. Is it acceptable for a Christian believer to date prior to getting married? The long and short answer is yes! It is generally acceptable for a Christian to date. Dating is a personal choice, different religious denominations and individuals may have varying views on dating practices. Many Christians believe in forming romantic relationships with the intention of marriage. In contrast, others may see dating as a way of getting to know someone before committing to a more serious relationship.

Before attempting to date, it is best to seek God in fasting and prayer concerning how and who you should date. Psalms 37:23-24 reads, *"The steps of a good man are ordered by the LORD: And he delighteth in his way. Though he fall, he shall not be utterly cast down: For the LORD upholds him with his hand."*[1] The Holy Spirit is concerned with every aspect of your life, he will guide you to the right person with whom he wants you to connect.

Some key factors to consider when dating as a Godly Christian include:
- What phase of life are you currently in?
- How are you handling the aging process?
- Do you feel like you are running out of time?
- Are you noticing changes in your youthful appearance?
- Do you experience feelings of isolation and loneliness?
- Are you experiencing hormonal changes?

Sexual Fantasy & The Christian Mind

Acknowledging these factors will aid in creating realistic expectations when dating. Research shows men peak sexually in their twenties and thirties, testosterone starts to slowly decrease around age thirty-five.[3] Studies indicate women reach their sexual peak in their late thirties and early forties. Studies also indicate women have more frequent intense sexual fantasies and are more likely to have sex earlier in a new relationship.[2] Understanding your body's dynamics before entering the world of dating is crucial for maintaining abstinence and gaining insight into the spiritual warfare you may experience while seeking to start a new courtship.

Let us explore the sexual aspect of your life during the dating phase. When getting to know someone, it is common for individuals to experience fluctuation in their sexual desires and temptations as time passes. However, born-again believers are encouraged to exercise self-control over their flesh, as advocated in Romans 12:1, *"which encourages believers to present their bodies as a living sacrifice to God."*[1] The enemy often infiltrates the Christian mind with sexual fantasies, aiming to cause frustration. True worship becomes elusive when the focus is lost, as emphasized in John 4:23-24, *"But the hour cometh and now is, when the true worshipers shall worship the Father in spirit and truth, for the Father seeketh such to worship Him."*[1]

The mental attacks are intended to disqualify you from being a genuine worshipper. In preparing for dating, it is crucial to rid your mind of biases against the opposite sex. Break free from erroneous beliefs, such as labeling all men as no good liars or assuming all women are gold diggers. Clearing such prejudicial thinking is a prerequisite for fostering long-term healthy relationships when seeking a potential partner.

Chapter Five: Godly Dating

HOW CAN I FIND SOMEONE?

In time past, people conversed openly in public without burying their heads in cell phones. Love connections were made at grocery stores, gas stations, lounges, churches, schools, cookouts, and more. Nowadays, your options are limited to meeting someone online or being set up on a blind date by a friend. You can also find a partner by making sure you are ready to date, if you are, God will guide them to you. If you are still struggling with lust, masturbation, sexual sin, low self-esteem, along with childhood traumas. You are not emotionally equipped to date, and it will be better for you to focus on getting delivered first.

If God allows you to find your spouse while still nursing an open wound, you will bleed all over that person, and as problems arise in your marriage, you will handle them in the flesh instead of the spirit. Also, if you continue dating in this state, you will attract broken, abusive, narcissistic, and toxic individuals. Their behavior will perpetuate the cycle of brokenness in your life. You will find someone when you are whole. Marriage is both a ministry and a business, you owe it to yourself to do the prep work before entering a union with someone. Some of you may disagree that marriage is a business. However, this perspective is evident in public divorce records.

By examining final court rulings, you will notice instances where couples are required to liquidate and divide their assets. If you are genuinely interested in finding a life partner and getting married, consider the following questions to evaluate your readiness for marriage. While these questions may appear extensive, intrusive, and intense, their purpose is not to question your worthiness for marriage. Instead, they are intended to assist you in preparing for a lifelong commitment by considering the bigger picture.

Sexual Fantasy & The Christian Mind

1. **How often do you pray?**
   Having a regular prayer life can guide you from resorting to worldly behaviors when addressing conflicts within your marriage.

2. **Are you truly devoted to God or religious?**
   Responding to issues with worldly reactions rather than spiritual ones can keep you trapped in a cycle of spiritual immaturity, hindering your growth.

3. **Are you a good communicator?**
   Effective communication with your spouse is crucial. Without it, you will be considered emotionally unavailable.

4. **Do you understand the responsibilities of being a Godly husband or wife?**
   The devil interferes with relationships and continuously accuses believers before God. If you are unsure what being a Godly spouse entails, you will be vulnerable to his attack. A husband is called to love his wife sacrificially, mirroring Christ's love for the church (Eph. 5.25-27).[1] A wife is to support her husband's God-given vision for their home, seeking guidance from God if she lacks clarity. Both partners should refrain from any form of abusive or hurtful speech towards each other, which can cause emotional instability and tension within the home.

Chapter Five: Godly Dating

5. **Do you feel the need to always have the last word?**
   It is essential to address this childish behavior before entering a marriage. Exercising restraint and remaining silent at times can be challenging yet necessary as an adult. Believing you are always right can lead to pride and arrogance in God's eyes. Eventually, this attitude will strain your relationship with your spouse and even lead to divorce.

6. **Are you selfish?**
   Focusing solely on yourself in a marriage does not work well in the long run. Over time, one partner may become exhausted from constantly accommodating the others' demands without their needs being met.

7. **Do you still blame your ex for the relationship not working out?**
   Are you still blaming your ex for the relationship not working out? Continuously blaming your ex shows that you have not reflected on your mistakes or taken responsibility for your actions. This behavior indicates a lack of maturity on your part. Remember, the breakdown of a relationship typically is fifty-fifty.

8. **Do you understand the role of being the head of the household?**
   What is the structure of a Godly household, and how should it be managed? A wise individual anticipates challenges and takes precautions. Do you intend to seek guidance from God regarding financial matters in your home? How frequently should you engage in prayer? What approach should you take to raising your children? Is it wise to store essential supplies in your garage?

9. **Do you know what it means to submit to your spouse?**
For women, submitting means recognizing that God has positioned your spouse as the head of your household, and they are responsible for maintaining the family's unity. However, this does not imply that your spouse should see you as inferior, as the Bible describes women as the "weaker vessel." Both your natural and spiritual contributions are equally important to the family's well-being and structure.

10. **Are you a workaholic?**
If you dedicate fourteen to sixteen hours daily to work, that leaves little time for nurturing relationships with others. Eventually, this imbalance may lead to neglecting your spouse and prioritizing your job over everything else, essentially turning it into an idol. You cannot enter marriage only to leave your partner alone at home. Your job is your spouse; the thing you spend the most time with is what has your heart, commitment, and affection.

11. **Are you active in ministry?**
If you seek a partner who shares your commitment to ministry, by demonstrating your involvement in church to potential candidates. This will allow them to see you working for God so they can make an informed decision about building a life with you. Revealing a call to ministry after marriage can lead to feelings of betrayal and strain the relationship.

Chapter Five: Godly Dating

12. Do you act like a child when things do not go your way?
Instead of handling challenges like an adult, do you resort to shutting down and giving people the silent treatment when upset? Do you react by swearing, yelling, breaking objects, or throwing things to make others take you seriously? This type of behavior will not work in a marriage.

13. Do you have bad spending habits?
It is crucial to know your monthly financial obligation; living by faith is admirable, but if you do so you consistently use your bill money on unnecessary items like clothing. You are falling short of being a good steward of God's blessing. Are you actively monitoring and managing your finances? If not, this imbalance could create challenges in a marriage, with one partner being a saver and the other a spender.

14. Are you overbearing & controlling?
Do you respect others' autonomy and allow them to make their own choices, or do you try to manipulate them into following your desires? When they resist your influence, do you punish them by withholding things? If these patterns resonate with you, it might be necessary to confront and seek deliverance from controlling behaviors. Manipulation is a sign of witchcraft.

Sexual Fantasy & The Christian Mind

15. Do you know how to combat the warfare that attacks a Godly marriage?
The power of agreement and covenant is what will keep the devil fighting against your marriage. One can chase a thousand, but two can chase ten thousand (*Deuteronomy 32:30*);[1] the union of your marriage threatens the kingdom of darkness. Your joining forces with another believer makes both of you a force to be reckoned with.

16. Do you possess the same qualities you seek in a spouse?
It is essential to stop demanding qualities you lack. If you are not clean, do not expect someone who values cleanliness to accept a messy living space. While it is natural to aim for improvement, fundamental life skills such as cooking, cleaning, financial responsibility, organization, and managing day-to-day tasks are vital for every adult. If you lack these skills, consider developing them while you wait for the right spouse; this will greatly enhance your marriage in the future.

17. Do you struggle with low self-esteem?
This issue is significant and often requires deliverance. When you have low self-worth, you may feel inadequate and constantly overcompensate by being excessively dramatic or not expressing your true self for fear of rejection. Insecurities can make you doubt your worthiness of love and lead to self-destructive behaviors, such as accusing the person you are dating of cheating on you with no solid proof. This usually happens when everything is going well, and you feel things are too good to be true.

Chapter Five: Godly Dating

18. Are you seeking marriage primarily for sexual reasons?
While the prospect of intimacy is exciting, it is necessary to recognize that sex is not the primary purpose of marriage. While sex is a part of marriage, it is only one component. Even in enjoying physical intimacy, it is important to maintain focus on the deeper reasons why God brought the two of you together.

19. Do you prioritize your family's opinions over God's guidance?
Despite aging physically, do you still rely on your family's choices rather than seeking God's direction in dating or marriage? It is essential to reflect on whether your family genuinely wants you to be happy. If they respect your relationship with God, they will trust the person God has approved for you to be with.

20. Do you understand the responsibility of taking on a spouse?
Have you counted the cost of having someone else in your personal space? Both of you will be occupying the same quarters, and when you want to be alone, they may want to be next to you.

Be honest with your answers; if you choose not to be, you are only lying to yourself. Give God something to work with. If you are in a place of singleness where you are hot and bothered, tell God the truth and ask for deliverance. It is hard to work for God when you are sexually frustrated.

Sexual Fantasy & The Christian Mind

Romans 12:2 reads, *"Therefore, I urge you, brothers, given God's mercy, to offer your bodies as living sacrifices, holy and pleasing to God—this is your spiritual act of worship. Do not conform any longer to the pattern of this world but be transformed by renewing your mind."*[1]

God did not call you for your sexuality he called you for his plan and purpose. You cannot allow these mind-controlling spirits to keep you in a place of not producing spiritual fruit. Get up from there and shake it off. You have work to do! This is the season you will win and overcome everything coming against you. But it will require some effort on your end; honesty is the key that will unlock the door to true deliverance. God wants you to live a victorious life in him, free of lust and all sexual sin.

Genesis 2:18-24 reads, *"And the LORD God said, "It is not good that man should be alone; I will make him a helper comparable to him." Out of the ground, the LORD God formed every beast of the field and every bird of the air and brought them to Adam to see what he would call them."*[1]

God wants to bless you with a spouse, not a sex slave. A Godly marriage is about two people coming together to do God's work. As the years pass in a marriage, your desire to have sex with your spouse diminishes due to varying factors. *"Only what you do for God will last (2 Corinthians 4:18)."*[1]

Chapter Five: Godly Dating

WHY AM I STILL SINGLE?

You are still single because you are married to a spirit spouse who will not permit you to marry anyone else until you repent of your sexual sins and get delivered through the blood of Jesus Christ. Once delivered, you must issue a divorce decree in the spirit realm. Another reason is romantic idealism. You immerse yourself in fairytales and romantic movies, waiting for your prince charming to sweep you off your feet so you can live happily ever after. Here is the ugly truth, there is no "happily ever after." This notation only exists in fairytales.

No one is coming on a white horse to sweep you off your feet, inflation is too high to afford a horse, and you may be afraid of heights. No man is going to run through the airport (with intense music playing in the background), shouting your name to grab your attention right before you board a plane. You turn around, locking eyes with him, dropping your purse and carry-on, then sprinting toward him with your hair blowing in the wind. As you jump into his arms, he takes a deep breath and says, "I love you, Barb. I am an idiot for not telling you sooner; I've been in love with you since the first day we met. "I'VE ALWAYS LOVED YOU AND I ALWAYS WILL! Then a big deep passionate kiss to end the scene"

Snap out of it and come back to reality! This cheesy scene is far from real. Who wants to risk their luggage and purse being stolen just to run into the arms of a man? Not to mention, airport security would have intervened since he bypassed the security checkpoints. There is nothing romantic about identity theft and handcuffs.

Sexual Fantasy & The Christian Mind

Timothy 3:1-5 reads, *"You should know this, Timothy, that in the last days, there will be tough times. People will be lovers of themselves and their money. They will be boastful and proud, scoffing at God, disobedient to their parents, and ungrateful. They will consider Nothing sacred."*[1]

So, why are you still single? You may be in love with yourself or dealing with one of the reasons listed below.

FEMALES & MALES

FEMALES
- Spirit Spouse
- Wrong Mindset
- Ms. Independent
- Waiting for Mr. 6'4
- Fear of Commitment
- Still dealing with Unresolved childhood Tramua
- Unwillingness to date outside your Race
- Seeking a wealthy Godly man to rescue you
- Unrealistic standards or expectations
- Fear of starting over with someone new
- Looking for a man with a title (Bishop, Prophet, Apostle)

MALES
- Spirit Spouse
- Fear of commitment
- Looking for the perfect BBL
- Emotionally Unavailable
- Not prepared to be a husband
- Fixating solely on the physical appearance
- Seeking short-term connections
- Still dealing with Unresolved childhood Tramua
- Unrealistic standards or expectations
- Unwillingness to socialize and build relationships
- Raised to be a son-husband still under your mother's full control

Chapter Five: Godly Dating

SINGLE & SAVED

Your number one responsibility as a single person is to work in ministry. God's word emphasized this because marriage is a ministry. Working with different personalities will help you gain a deeper understanding of ministering to a spouse. Furthermore, you will discover areas that require further development while interacting with others. God will use the people you work with in ministry to be your sandpaper, not to mention he may use ministry to put you in touch with your spouse. So, instead of feeling sorry for yourself because you are still single, choose to start working in ministry.

It is okay to desire marriage, but God does not want you to be fixated on marriage to the point where it demobilizes you. Leaving you in a compromised position where you struggle with sexual fantasies. A Godly marriage will require you to have a servant's heart. Doing ministry work is the best way to obtain a heart of servitude which brings on the spirit of humility. Individuals need to align their dating practices with their personal beliefs and values. Many Christians seek to date consistent with their faith, which may involve shared values, mutual respect, and a commitment to maintaining moral and ethical standards in their relationships.

Ultimately, whether dating is considered appropriate for a Christian is a matter of personal conviction, and individuals should seek guidance from their faith community, religious leaders, and personal reflection when making dating decisions. It is essential to discern the true intentions of the person you are dating at the start of the relationship.

Sexual Fantasy & The Christian Mind

EMBRACING SINGLENESS IN MINISTRY

Let us address a topic often avoided in religious circles the single life, ministry work, and the unexpected presence of sexual fantasies. Despite the silence surrounding these issues, it is time to have an open conversation about navigating singleness while serving in ministry. Being single in ministry offers unique trials for believers striving to honor God. While focused on saving souls, leading worship, or guiding youth groups, there is often a lingering voice in your mind urging you to find a partner, settle down, and create the perfect ministry family.

However, this script is outdated, not to mention the pressure from older members of the faith asking, "When are you going to settle down?" Prioritizing kingdom work above your desires often feels overwhelming. Living single while serving in ministry can feel like a rollercoaster. One moment, you feel content in your singleness, the next you desire companionship, especially when facing the nuances of ministry. As time goes on, the struggle wears down your resolve, leading you to compromise your standards by giving in to your sexual desires.

Unintentionally, the modern-day church leaves single Christians feeling inferior due to their material status. Being single in ministry is a stop on the way to marriage, and although it feels as if it is taking forever for you to get married, the love and support of a church community can impact your attitude while waiting on God's timing. Whether you are in leadership, the music ministry, or the tech whiz behind the Sunday morning livestream, your singleness does not detract from your ability to serve and make a meaningful impact on the congregation.

Chapter Five: Godly Dating

Serving in ministry allows you to connect with people in ways you never imagined. Remember this, your singleness will not last forever so embrace it while you can. Celebrate the freedom it affords you and recognize that you are on track for a "suddenly" relationship. Your singleness is a powerful asset in your ministry toolkit, and when God leads you to the right person, you will be the answer to their prayers. They will not waste time playing games, things will happen fast and in God's divine order.

"The least of you will become a thousand, the smallest a mighty nation. I am the LORD; in its time I will do this swiftly" (Isaiah 60:22).[1]

BREAKING THE STIGMA

While you are waiting on God to move on your behalf, in the meantime, you have the power to break the stigma attached to single Christians in ministry. Somehow, the assumption is that singles are incomplete, that there is a missing piece only marriage can fill. Newsflash, your singleness is not a problem waiting for a solution. Confront these outdated notions and break this stigma. You are effective, passionate, and committed to your calling. Your relationship status does not define your ability to serve or your worthiness in the eyes of God. The life of a single Christian comes with its fair share of loneliness.

Balancing ministry commitments with the desire for companionship is not easy. It is okay to acknowledge the occasional pangs of loneliness but do not let it overshadow the fulfilling aspects of your singleness. Build a strong support network within your ministry community.

"Set your affection on things above, not on things on the earth" (Colossians 3:2).[1]

Sexual Fantasy & The Christian Mind

This will help you to cast down sexual thoughts before they turn into actions. Surround yourself with friends who can relate to what you are going through involving the joys and quirks of being single in ministry. Loneliness can be a powerful motivator for deepening your connection with God. Keep the focus on saving souls and overcoming sexual fantasies. Being single, working in church, and having a vivid imagination can affect your performance in ministry by opening the door for you to lust more when interacting with others. Dealing with sexual sins can make you a ministry misfit.

Acknowledging this shortcoming does not mean you are signing up for a guilt trip. But God does want you to rid yourself of sin so, your gift can be used in its purest form. He does not want you to normalize your experiences as a natural part of the human experience. God knows you are cased in the flesh, but Jesus overcame all fleshly deeds and gave you the power to do the same. Whether it is taking control of your thoughts during a sermon or ceasing to daydream during service, remember you can put on the helmet of salvation to prevent these thoughts from entering your mind.

SPIRITUAL WELL-BEING

God knows that you have been single for a long time, and with each passing year, your hope of meeting someone dwindles. But even in this state, he still wants you to have balance in your spirituality and your sexuality. God designed your body. He is the one that hard-wired you for sex; he is also aware that as your body changes with age, you may have a greater need for sex depending on your hormone levels. Recognizing that both aspects are valid and do not have to be at odds is essential. Balancing spiritual and sexual well-being is about acknowledging your desires without compromising your commitment to your faith. Incorporating practices that nurture both aspects of your life.

Chapter Five: Godly Dating

Engage in prayer, meditation, and spiritual reflection to maintain your connection with your faith. Simultaneously, step out of your comfort zone by getting out more and spending time with friends and family. Your work in ministry is commendable, but God does not want you walking a tightrope between sex and faith, he wants you to find the equilibrium needed that will fulfill your life in ministry.

LONG COURTSHIP

As you embark on the journey of dating as a single Christian, be sure to establish an acceptable time frame for the longevity of your relationship at the beginning. Dating someone for one, maybe two years without a marital commitment is allowable, but anything beyond this time frame becomes high risk. A long-drawn-out courtship will make it difficult for both parties to abstain from becoming sexually active, the more affectionate you become towards one another, the more you will long to be closer. When you are apart, you will find yourself missing your love interest; during this time, the thoughts of sexual fantasies will creep in.

Although you may try your best to keep it PG-13, the physical attraction you both feel for each other will take things to an "R" rating. Having healthy boundaries is an excellent way to safeguard your relationship, sexing your way to the altar is not the right way to enter a marriage. Establishing boundaries in Christian dating is crucial for maintaining a healthy and God-honoring relationship.

Sexual Fantasy & The Christian Mind

Here is a list of potential boundaries that you should consider having in place.

Purity in Physical Boundaries:
- Avoid tongue kissing, this can lead to fornication.
- Avoid being home alone with the person (No "Netflix and chill").
- Try to avoid grabbing body parts or excessive touching.
- Be mindful of how you hug the person.

Emotional Boundaries:
- Taking time to gradually build an emotional connection.
- Being mindful of emotional involvement and attachment.
- Avoid telling the person your whole life story in one day.
- Refrain from leaning on the person for emotional support.

Communication Boundaries:
- Honest and open communication about expectations.
- Discussing feelings and concerns respectfully.
- Setting boundaries for communication frequency and methods.
- It is best NOT to spend hours on the phone, you have your whole life to get to know this person. There is no need to rush the process.

Spiritual Boundaries:
- Prioritizing shared faith, values, and beliefs matters.
- Committing to spiritual growth individually and as a couple.
- Praying together and for each other.

Chapter Five: Godly Dating

Time Boundaries:
- Balancing time spent together with other commitments.
- Respecting each other's time and space.
- Avoid excessive isolation from friends and family.

Accountability Boundaries:
- Seeking guidance and accountability from mentors or a faith community.
- Being open to feedback and constructive criticism.
- Encouraging a culture of accountability within the relationship.

Modesty Boundaries:
- Making modest choices in clothing and behavior.
- Respecting each other's bodies and personal space.
- Upholding a sense of dignity and self-respect.

Financial Boundaries:
- Being transparent about financial situations and goals.
- Setting boundaries on spending and financial decisions for courtship.
- Collaborating on financial planning if the relationship becomes more serious.

Family Boundaries:
- Being respectful and considerate of each other's families.
- Establishing expectations for involvement with extended family.
- Communicating openly about family dynamics and expectations.

Future Boundaries:
- o Discussing long-term goals and plans.
- o Setting expectations for the future of the relationship.
- o Being honest about your intentions regarding marriage and commitment.

When setting boundaries, it is important to recognize your areas of vulnerability. What are your sexual triggers that will cause you to fall out of God and into bed with someone? What actions or situations quickly get you horny and aroused? Identifying these pleasure sensors allows you to avoid them altogether. Life often involves a series of actions and reactions, if kissing, touching, cuddling, being alone with someone in a romantic setting, fingering, intimate close physical hugs, or fondling makes you feel hot and bothered, it is crucial to establish boundaries to avoid these situations. Couples need to communicate openly, establish these boundaries together, and regularly revisit them to ensure that they are aligned with the values and goals of the relationship. Additionally, seeking guidance from trusted mentors or spiritual leaders can provide valuable insights.

THE RIGHT ONE

Only God can reveal if you are connecting with the person he intended for you to be with. Unfortunately, as a Christian, you are constantly engaged in spiritual warfare, and the *"weapons of our warfare are not carnal but mighty through God by the pulling down of strongholds"* (2 Corinthians 10:4).[1]

Chapter Five: Godly Dating

When it is time for you to marry, you will always face the conundrum of who to choose. God will present you with his offer, and so will the devil (this is called a counterfeit spirit). It is a man or woman who appears to be your ideal mate by checking all the boxes on your list. This person could also be a believer who is stuck in a phase of spiritual immaturity. Despite having been in Christ for some time, they show minimal growth and tend to operate from a place of carnality. This spiritual stagnation makes them susceptible to being influenced and used by the enemy.

The enemy works his enchantment by executing a plan and strategy in your life, the person he sends your way will appeal to all your senses above your waist and below. The devil keeps a record of your preferences for the opposite sex and knows precisely what you like. His objective is to persuade you into marrying the wrong person, a choice that could detour your ministry, impact your destiny, and weaken your spiritual defenses. Getting married to the wrong person has the potential to cause significant harm, leading to years of suffering that will require you to rebuild your life from the ashes. Once they divorce you and walk away.

Satan will use this agent of darkness to drag you through a nasty, messy divorce where they will take everything, drag your name through the mud, and ruin your reputation. Leaving you for dead. God's word reads, *"One can chase a thousand, but two can chase ten thousand"* (Deuteronomy 32:30).[1] This is called the power of agreement, which is why he attacks relationships.

The Bible reads, *"Let two walk together because if one falls, the other will be able to help the other one up"* (Ecclesiastes 4:10).[1]

Sexual Fantasy & The Christian Mind

When selecting a life partner, be sure to seek God's guidance. Your chosen partner should embody the qualities described in 1 Corinthians 13:4-7: *Love is patient, Love is kind. It does not envy, it does not boast, it is not proud. It does not dishonor others; it is not self-seeking, is not easily angered, and keeps no record of wrongs. Godly Love does not delight in evil but rejoices with the truth. It always protects, always trusts, always hopes, always perseveres.*[1] Love, as depicted in these verses, is the essential component needed for the sustainability and longevity of a marriage.

Pay close attention to their actions to ensure they are adding to your life in a good way. If their presence in your life starts distracting you from the things of God. They have been sent to tear you down and stop you dead in your tracks. Observe how they treat others, listen to their conversations. If you let a person talk long enough, they will tell on themselves. Often people reveal their true nature through their words. Do they uplift and celebrate others? Are they focused on living holy and working in ministry? Do not allow the excitement of a new relationship to blind your eyes, block your spiritual discernment, or cloud your judgment.

If you are serious about the call of God on your life. Take the time to evaluate your situation to ensure you are connecting with someone who is a destiny helper and is in alignment with your spiritual growth and development rather than hindering it. A counterfeit person is the personification of all you desire in a spouse, but their true intention is to lead you astray. As a result of this, you will find yourself experiencing an increase in sexual fantasies, weakening your resolve and pushing you towards operating in the spirit of lust. Their goal is to defile you through the spirit of sexual perversion and to get you off course by getting you to engage in sinful sexual acts.

They may present themselves as holy, kind, nurturing, and sweet, even giving the impression that serving God is their top priority. However, it is all a façade. They are merely putting on a show to win you over. If you marry this person, you will begin seeing their true colors after the wedding.

Chapter Five: Godly Dating

That is when you will discover they lack a genuine prayer life or commitment to spiritual disciplines. They inconsistently attend church and have a problem with authority. They are materialistic, superficial, egotistical, demanding, selfish, narcissistic, controlling, and rude—the best way for a Christian to vet a counterfeit spouse while dating is to check their fruits. A genuine person of faith will not feel the need to impress you. Instead, they will be their authentic self because they are looking for someone to accept them for who they truly are.

Conversely, an agent of darkness will push for sexual intimacy or marriage early on in the relationship by doing everything they can to get you in bed or to the alter as quickly as possible. This is because their fakeness typically lasts only six to twelve months before revealing their true character. They know having sex with you will impair your judgment and create a mind fog by letting in mind-controlling spirits. If you genuinely desire a relationship with a true man or woman of God. Why entertain such carnality? Entangling yourself with an agent of darkness will create recurring cycles of setbacks in your life, delaying your ministry and slowing your spiritual growth.

You might find yourself expressing frustration, saying, "I'm tired of this always happening to me." Proverbs 13:12 reads, "Hope deferred makes the heart sick." If you want to break this cycle, then STOP! Giving time and energy to prioritizing the things of the flesh over the things of God. Remember, you are sons and daughters of the Most High God, and you should always conduct yourselves accordingly. The person God sent to you is not in a hurry to get you to the bedroom. They have no desire to control you.

Another way you can tell God's choice from the devil's is to put them in situations outside the realm of traditional dating such as going bowling, skating, rock climbing, painting, and top golf. This will put them in situations where they are not in control, you can then sit back and observe their behavior.

Sexual Fantasy & The Christian Mind

God's choice may be a diamond in the rough outwardly, but inwardly, they possess everything you need in a spouse. They were sent to improve your quality of life and help you build in ministry. The unfortunate reality is many Christians end up marrying someone who is sent to lead them away from God instead of the one sent to help them build in God. This happens because they place more emphasis on physical attributes, such as appearance, over spiritual discernment, especially when operating from a place of carnality. Christian believers fall into the trap of choosing a partner based solely on looks, height, and body shape.

When a child of God settles for an imposter, it impacts the body of Christ significantly. The realm of darkness operates like a vacuum, gradually sucking you in and stripping you of your spiritual strength and ability to resist the enemy. Once it consumes you entirely, you will find yourself entangled in spiritual warfare, requiring the assistance of spiritual leaders, elders, and mentors to pull you out. Rescuing a Christian who has fallen for the enemy's deceit consumes valuable time away from other areas of ministry. A failed attempt can leave them feeling overwhelmed with guilt and despair, causing them to distance themselves from God altogether.

In Genesis 29:1, God promised Jacob he would become the father of the twelve tribes of Israel. With his mother's help, he stole his brother's birthright, prompting her to send him to his uncle's house for his safety. On his way there he met his first cousin Rachel, who was beautiful and captivating. It was lust at first sight. When he met his uncle (without seeking God to find out if Rachel was his wife). He inquired of her bride price, his uncle told him that he would have to work seven years for her hand in marriage. He was so in lust with her, that he counted the time as child's play. At the end of the seven years, he told his uncle, "Give me my wife so that I may lay with her."

He did not say to grow old with her or spend time with her but "lay with her (Genesis 29:21-22), "[1] his uncle agreed to his request. During the marriage ceremony, he intoxicated Jacob with wine, and he then sent in his eldest daughter, Leah. When Jacob woke up the next day, he was mad when he discovered what his uncle had done

Chapter Five: Godly Dating

His uncle told him, "In our culture, it is not customary for the younger sister to marry before the elder." Jacob asked what it would cost to get Rachel, to which his uncle replied, "It will take another seven years." Filled with lust and anger, he agreed to work an additional seven years for Rachel's hand in marriage. In the meantime, he despised Leah because she was not as beautiful as her sister. After completing the second set of seven years, Jacob told his uncle. "Give me my wife that I may lay with her." His uncle finally granted his request, and God, seeing that Leah was despised, opened her womb for her to have children.

Leah and her handmaiden bore Jacob eight out of the twelve tribes of Israel. Rachel and her handmaiden bore four. The moral of the story is God's choice will help you accomplish your destiny. He has ordained them to be the multiplier in your life. In the end, Jacob was married to four women, and his choice was the weakest link. She tried to get him to serve other gods and idols. She only gave him two of the twelve tribes, and she died giving birth to the second child, which she named "Benoni, meaning sorrow and pain."[1] Jacob renamed him Benjamin, meaning son of the right hand (Genesis 35:16-18).[1]

The fact that she gave the child a bitter name while knocking on death's door lets you know she did not respect authority. In those days, it was the man who named his son and spoke a blessing over him, not the woman. You are responsible for seeking God in prayer and fasting to discern if you are connecting to the right person. You should not marry someone just because you think they are a good man or good woman; they may not be your good man or good woman. Your spouse's assignment is to be a helpmate to you, the same as you are to them. Let God show you if the person you are dating is the right fit for you long-term. The purpose of a Godly marriage is for both of you to serve in ministry. Getting married to the wrong person will ultimately prove to be disastrous in the end.

Sexual Fantasy & The Christian Mind

You may be tired of being alone and feel as if you are ready to date. However, before taking matters into your own hands:

- ➢ Seek God in prayer and fasting to find out who he has in store for you.

- ➢ Bind up all counterfeit spirits from finding you.

- ➢ If you find yourself drowning in sexual fantasies over the person you fell in lust with ask God to deliver you.

- ➢ Send the counterfeit back to the pits of hell from whence they came.

Individuals who practice witchcraft will appear in your dreams to have sex with you prior to meeting. This is to form a sexual soul tie. So, when they meet you in person, you cannot resist them. A true man of God will take you by your hand and lead you to the altar before leading you to the bedroom, a true woman of God knows her worth. She values her body and will not use it as a down payment on a ring. God's choice is more concerned with your performance outside the bedroom than within it.

OUT WITH THE OLD IN WITH THE NEW

Dating is complicated, and remaining in touch with an ex gives them direct access to sabotage your future. These individuals do not want you, but they do not want anyone else to have you. They are on assignment to frustrate your life and keep you off balance. Unless children are involved, there is no need to remain in contact with your ex. The enemy may have sent your ex to keep you in a place of stuck. This includes individuals you meet on dating apps.

Chapter Five: Godly Dating

They do not want to date you or get married but want to remain friends. Did you go on a dating app or a virtual pen pal app? The answer is "NO!" You are looking for something long-term that leads to marriage. Your singleness is like a parking spot. Some will assume the spot is taken if you allow friends to occupy the space. Many of you desire to have what your grandparents have. Stop coveting your parents' or grandparents' marriage because you are not willing to roll up your sleeves and do the work they did to keep it together. In today's vain society, where a relationship is built primarily on appearance, you are not willing to date someone who looks like a younger version of your parents or grandparents.

Stop wasting time dating individuals out of desperation. If you settle for someone out of loneliness and impatience, you will create your version of hell on earth and may wind up divorced. When a Christian marries someone who is not on the same spiritual level, that person becomes a target for the devil. The enemy attacks the weakest link in a relationship. The devil will constantly work through this person because they have no idea how to protect their gates. Their inability to fight him off will give the enemy an all-access pass to your life courtesy of your spouse. You will live in a constant state of turmoil because they lack an in-depth understanding of spiritual warfare.

A BETTER OPTION

Any person who does not want to marry you after one or two years of dating has no intentions of being with you long-term. You are nothing more than a placeholder until someone better comes along, and when that better option shows up, you will see their wedding pictures on social media in less than six months Adding insult to injury, that person will reappear in your life after being married for only three months hoping you will forgive them and agree to be their "side chic" or "boy toy."

Sexual Fantasy & The Christian Mind

If you agree to this arrangement by investing your time, love, and affection, the devil has you right where he wants you living beneath your Christian values. Forfeiting your birthright for momentary pleasures. The lasting effects of your sexual sin will transcend through generations. If you remain in this state, it will alter the trajectory of your life. This adulterous act will also dry up your finances and tie up resources in both of your lives. Leaving you hopeless and helpless, unable to feel God's presence, this sinful action will lead you down a path of believing God has turned his back on you. The person who wants to grow old with you will take you off the market as quickly as possible without hesitating or second-guessing themselves.

THEY BELONG TO THE STREETS

It is acceptable if someone you are considering dating is not interested in marriage, but before getting romantically involved with this person, it is important to understand that a person in their late thirties, forties, or fifties who adamantly refuses marriage will not commit to a serious relationship and might be better suited for casual encounters. They belong to the streets. Instead of compromising your integrity to prove to them that you are wife or husband material. Walk away! Their heart is fixed, and their mind is made up. Respect their truth and stick to your non-negotiables.

This is an agent of darkness who will ask you to perform every profane sexual act under the sun; it will be sixty shades of gray instead of fifty. They will see you as a lonely, desperate individual (a man-pleaser) who is willing to do anything for love. This includes compromising your stance in God. They will have you doing everything married people do and will enjoy all the benefits of your hard work. Once they are done using you like a napkin. They will look you straight in the eye, laugh, and say, "And you call yourself a Christian, yeah, right!" This person will never see your worth because you allowed them to devalue you.

Chapter Five: Godly Dating

If you permit them, they will string you along for years with no commitment. A sexless relationship is not an option with such an individual. Knowing how to choose the right partner is essential to Godly dating. Not everyone who professes to be a Christian is trustworthy. Do not allow anyone to remain in your life with ungodly dating practices. Such individuals will undermine your desire to married. Remove them from your life if you are serious about finding a Godly spouse, recognize your value, and adjust your mindset accordingly. Dealing with this agent of darkness can deeply impact your self-esteem. Leaving you feeling emotionally drained, struggling with their rejection of you and your own feelings of self-rejection.

This person is controlling, and the same qualities that first attracted you to them are now causing you distress. Initially, they seemed confident and assertive, but as time passed, you started noticing their selfish, narcissistic behavior. The most effective way to break free from this toxic individual is to sever all ties by cutting them loose. Dating an individual so dogmatic will inevitably diminish your sense of self-worth. This person is intoxicating, and keeping your distance from them requires effort. Put your hands in God's and take it one day at a time. You got this!

Proverbs 18:22 says, *"For he that findeth a wife findeth a good thing and shall obtain favor in the sight of God."*[1]

The breakdown of this scripture is that when two God-ordained people find each other, they both benefit. The husband is endowed with supernatural divine favor, and the wife receives her covering, allowing her to feel safe and protected. You were created in the likeness and image of God. He ordained you to be his mouthpiece on earth before he placed you in your mother's womb. God did not create you to be anyone's jump-off station, boy toy, or hot-line bling representative. You were created for greater, it is time to end this destructive cycle of settling for the wrong person.

Sexual Fantasy & The Christian Mind

SEX BEFORE MARRIAGE

2 Corinthians 6:17-18 reads, *"Wherefore Come out from among them, and be ye separate, saith the Lord, And touch not the unclean thing; And I will receive you, And will be a Father unto you, And ye shall be my sons and daughters, saith the Lord Almighty."*[1]

As Christian believers, we are the blueprint for holy living on earth, our commission is to show unbelievers that living, a sanctified, set-apart life for God while on earth is possible. We know the only righteous one is God, 1 Corinthians 5:21 tells us,

"We are declared righteous, and fully accepted by God, not based on any righteousness in us, but only through faith, looking outside ourselves and joining us to a righteousness, not of our own doing — Jesus who is our righteousness."[1]

Your Heavenly Father wants the clean, holy, set apart, pure version of you. Having sex with multiple partners in hopes of getting an "I Do" is not his will for your life. This is an illegal way to enter marriage, and it will not last because you are building your house on sand instead of a firm foundation. I know the world believes in test driving the car before buying one, but too many of you have gone from a test to an exam. You have been tried and tested repeatedly with no down payment or serious buyers. You are selling yourself short by allowing others to use and abuse you. You have done the sexting and phone sex in addition to compromising your morals by sleeping around with different partners.

Where is the ring for all your hard work? Now, here you are marinating in your singleness wondering when? God said in his word he would be a father to you, and you will be his sons and daughters. A good father solely wants the best for his children but will only give it to them when they are mature enough to handle it.

Sexual Fantasy & The Christian Mind

Abstaining from sex as a single Christian is possible, but you must keep your eyes on God, by avoiding carnality, keeping your flesh on the altar, and offering your body as a living sacrifice (Romans 12:1). Bringing your body under subjection is intentional. You cannot make excuses like "I 'm not perfect, I'm human, God understands." It is not about God's understanding. Do you understand that the wages of sin is death (Romans 6:23)? Proverbs 14:12 reads, *"There is a way which seemeth right unto a man, But the end thereof are the ways of death."*[1]

Stop making excuses for your flesh! After reading the previous chapters in this book, you should have a better understanding of the level of warfare in which you have been engaged. No more being lukewarm! It is either you come out of sin or stay in, but if you die and your soul be lost, "it ain't nobody's fault but yours."

SINGLENESS AND THE CHURCH

In the last thirty years, there has been a significant decline in Christian marriages, marking an era where a considerable number of church leaders are single. A notable trend in today's churches is the increasing recruitment of women over men in the church, leading to an apparent imbalance within the household of faith. Weekends are often filled with numerous women-centered activities such as workshops, prayer meetings, empowerment sessions, retreats, and events. This is creating a disproportion where the male ministry is notably absent in many congregations.

This unfolding development is reshaping the modern-day church, giving rise to a perception that it resembles more of a social networking club. Where female believers gather to worship and engage in professional networking. Like other social institutions, the church sometimes struggles with understanding singleness.

Sexual Fantasy & The Christian Mind

Many individuals navigating single life often find themselves caught in a paradox surrounded by a community preaching love and acceptance, yet inadvertently marginalizing those who are not a part of a traditional family unit. This raises the question, does the church unintentionally prioritize married couples and families over singles? In most churches, the absence of a dedicated singles ministry exacerbates the issue. Particularly single men, who are often lacking the pre-marital advice needed for choosing the right spouse or becoming Godly husbands. Coupled with the neglect of leadership not fostering the males' spiritual growth.

This leaves many men feeling inadequate and subsequently leads to them marrying outside of their faith because the church's focus is on empowering women. New-age Christian men feel as if they are unable to match the spiritual level of modern-day Christian women. Stereotypes surrounding Christian singles often stem from a limited perspective of the community, influenced by media representations and societal biases. The church must challenge these stereotypes to eradicate sexism and create balance in the body of Christ. Church leaders should take more initiative to encourage singles to connect within the church body.

Achieving balance and support is critical for those seeking a Godly spouse. There should be just as many workshops for men as there are for women, ensuring that both genders receive equal attention and guidance. Recognizing that families are the cornerstone of society and allocating additional resources to the singles ministry is essential. This investment will aid in creating more families and strengthening the church in the long run.

Chapter Five: Godly Dating

HOLD ON, DO NOT LOSE HOPE!

Living life as a single Christian is no easy feat, it is certainly not for the faint of heart. Regardless of your relationship status, recognize that your singleness is temporary. Ecclesiastes 3:1 in the Bible reminds us, *"There is a time for everything and a season for every activity under the heavens."*[1] The temporariness of your situation appears realistic and long-term, but that is not the truth despite the enemy's attempts to make you believe you will remain single forever. The body of Christ is comprised of single men and women of diverse ages, ethnicities, and cultures. There are assorted options available. While these options may not be immediately evident in your local church, they exist within the broader community of believers.

The devil knows that God wants you to be married, but ultimately, whether you marry or die alone is up to you. He wants to keep you in a state of singleness by using the legal right you gave him through sexual immorality to frustrate you. The devil knows that when you are tired and frustrated with being single, you might become desperate and consider pursuing a relationship with someone of the same sex, believing it could be your only opportunity to find love. You have been single longer than most people have been married, but Your spirit man is prompting you to hold on and not lose hope. The Holy Spirit encourages you to stand on God's promise and believe his word. He wants you to SPRING into action and take control of your destiny by remaining steadfast in his word. God heard your prayers, and he sees your tears. He will bring you out, and you will rejoice as you enter your new season of open doors and new opportunities.

Chapter Six
Sexual Fantasy and Your Marriage
Marriage is a Ministry

Marriage is a ministry and should be approached accordingly. It is a union between two individuals entering a spiritual covenant with God. (Ecclesiastes 4:*12) reads, "A threefold cord is not easily broken."*[1] Marriage is more than a legal contract binding two individuals together. It is a ministry that requires dedication, commitment, and a profound understanding of its significance in the lives of those involved. Standing at the altar, the bride and groom are poised to start a new chapter of life that extends beyond the honeymoon phase and into everyday living. The significance of this moment is underscored by their reflection on the dating process—the highs, the lows, and the shared experiences that have shaped the bond between them.

As a ministry, marriage requires a practical dimension beyond societal norms and expectations. It involves a commitment to nurturing a partnership that goes beyond the individual needs of each spouse. The concept of ministry implies a sense of service, care, and a shared purpose that extends beyond personal gratification. It involves recognizing each partner's role in supporting and uplifting the other. Marriage, much like any ministry, has its challenges. The devil desires to break up your marriage and turn both of you against each other. He achieves this by targeting your psyche.

Sexual Fantasy & The Christian Mind

Once he gains entry to your mind, he proceeds to weaken your emotional barriers, enticing you to stray from your marital commitment by indulging in sexual fantasies. Keeping a marriage together requires resilience, a willingness to adapt, and the understanding that growth often comes through shared experiences. Just as a ministry involves devotion to a higher purpose, marriage calls for a dedication to the shared goals and aspirations of the couple. It recognizes the sacred nature of the commitment made at the altar and calls for a mindset surpassing the relationship's superficial exterior.

The transitions from dating to the wedding day services as a testament to the choices, efforts, and shared experiences that shape the narrative of the couple's life together. Entering a marriage with a ministry mindset ensures that the union is a lifelong commitment to the shared growth of two souls bound together.

EXCHANGE OF VOWS

"Dearly beloved, we are gathered here today (tonight) to join this man and this woman in holy matrimony." Groom's name_____, do you take this woman to be your wife, to live together in holy matrimony, to love her, to honor her, to comfort her, and to keep her in sickness and in health, forsaking all others, for as long as you both shall live?" do you take this man to be your husband, to live together in holy matrimony, to love him, to honor him, to comfort him, and to keep him in sickness and in health, forsaking all others, for as long as you both shall live?" "I, Groom's name_____, take you Bride's name_____, to be my wife, to have and to hold from this day forward, for better, for worse, for richer, for poorer, in sickness and in health, to love and to cherish, till death do us part."

Chapter Six: Sexual Fantasy & Your Marriage

The notary asks the man to place the ring on the woman's finger and to repeat the following, "I give you this ring as a token and pledge of our constant faith and abiding love." The notary asks the couple to join hands, then declares, "By virtue of the authority vested in me under the laws of the State of _____, I now pronounce you husband and wife." To the man: "You may kiss the bride.

WHAT IS A VOW?

A vow is a solemn promise to do a specified thing.[2] When you exchanged your wedding vows, you promised to "forsake all others." This means leaving behind old habits and ways of thinking. Now that you have committed to marriage with a natural spouse, it is time to break the vows you made with your spirit spouse. The following verses are a reminder of what God expects of you when you make a vow.

Psalm 50:14
"Offer to God a sacrifice of thanksgiving.
And pay your vows to the Most High;[1]

Job 22:27
"You will pray to Him, and He will hear you;
And you will pay your vows.[1]

Ecclesiastes 5:5
When you make a vow to God, do not be late in paying it; for He takes no delight in fools. Pay what you vow! It is better that you should not vow than that you should vow and not pay.[1]

Sexual Fantasy & The Christian Mind

Deuteronomy 23:21
"When you make a vow to the Lord your God, you shall not delay to pay it, for it would be sin in you, and the Lord your God will surely require it of you. [1]

A woman or man who makes a vow without fully understanding the gravity of their obligation may break that vow shortly after it has been made. Honoring your marriage vow will strengthen the bounds of your union.. Central to this bond is the wedding vows—a solemn promise exchanged between partners in the presence of witnesses. While modern society sometimes downplays the significance of cherishing your vows. It is important for the health and longevity of your marriage. Honoring wedding vows sets a positive example for future generations.

Children raised in households where faithfulness and integrity are prioritized are more likely to carry these values into their relationships. By modeling a healthy and respectful marriage, couples inspire others to prioritize their vows and invest in the well-being of their relationship. In a culture with high divorce rates, honoring wedding vows becomes even more critical to protecting the sanctity of marriage. It reaffirms the sacredness of fidelity and underscores the significance of a lifelong partnership. By upholding their promise, couples deepen their bond, set a positive tone for the future, and contribute to preserving the institution of marriage.

MARRIAGE IS A MINISTRY

During your years of singleness, your focus was on ministry, which may have caused you to fall prey to the devil's trap. Loneliness, aloneness, and isolation from doing ministry by yourself may have gotten the better of you, causing you to have a few slip-ups along the way. Lust stepped in and took over your mind during a time when you were spiritually drained from doing the Lord's work.

Chapter Six: Sexual Fantasy & Your Marriage

The erotic fantasies you had at night provided a way of escape that rescued you from the state of being alone. Now that you are married, you will need to use your ministerial training to overcome the spirit of sexual perversion in your marriage. Providing your training is in line with God's word. Marriage is the second most important ministry you will have on the earth.

Ephesians 5:22-25)reads, *"Wives, to submit to their husbands as to the Lord...Husbands love your wives, just as Christ loved the church. He gave up his life for her."* [1]

A newly married man has no idea how to embody this scripture except by the leading of the Holy Spirit. A man develops Godly love in his heart towards his wife over time. This level of loving his wife, to the point where he is willing to die for her, requires selflessness and self-discipline. This kind of love will grow each time he ministers to her through acts of kindness and words of affirmation, even when she gets on his nerves. The process of a woman submitting to her husband is continuous and tends to become easier as time passes and trust deepens. Similarly to her learning how to follow the guidance of her natural and spiritual father, she must also learn to embrace her husband's leadership.

However, for a woman who grew up without a father or had a strained relationship with her spiritual father, accepting the idea of submission may prove challenging. Consequently, she might perceive herself as inferior to her husband rather than recognizing their equality. Modern-day Christianity has done an excellent job of distorting the genuine concept of a woman submitting to her husband. The term "woman" itself suggests the role of being a "womb-man," one who gives birth to the vision in the relationship, she is the multiplier.

Sexual Fantasy & The Christian Mind

While God entrusts the vision to the husband as the head of the household, it is often the woman whom God employs to bring that vision to fruition. Every man's vision has been nurtured and birth by a woman, be it a grandmother, aunt, sister, girlfriend, best friend, teacher, or mentor. It is through the support and encouragement of a woman that a man evolves into a better version of himself to fulfill God's divine mandate on his life. So, what does any of this have to do with sexual fantasies? In moments within a marriage where one partner feels inferior, misunderstood, or insecure, the instinctual response of the mind is to seek an escape route.

Often, this leads to withdrawal from your spouse to avoid confrontation which leaves you inadvertently seeking refuge in the familiar. Before you know it, you are back in the arms of the enemy, engaging in weird sexual warfare. Just as ministers collaborate in their work to serve their congregations, spouses should unite in their marriage to support each other and their community. This partnership involves sharing joys, successes, and facing setbacks together, providing strength and encouragement to one another along the way. Moreover, marriage as a ministry emphasizes the importance of selflessness and sacrifice.

Just as religious leaders often put the needs of others before their own, spouses in a marriage ministry prioritize the well-being and happiness of their partner. This might mean making compromises, offering forgiveness, or simply being there to listen and support without judgment. This will keep your spouse out of the arms of their spirit spouse and in yours. When the devil tries to sneak into your marriage, communicate with your spouse so both of you can pray together. Communication plays a vital role in the ministry of marriage. Effective communication fosters understanding, empathy, and intimacy between partners.

Chapter Six: Sexual Fantasy & Your Marriage

It allows them to express their needs, fears, and dreams openly, by creating a safe space for vulnerability and growth. Through communication, couples can navigate conflicts, deepen their connection, and strengthen their bond as they work together towards common goals. In addition to nurturing their relationship, couples engaged in the ministry of marriage also have the opportunity to extend their love and support to others.

It is important to acknowledge that the ministry of marriage has its challenges. Like any ministry, it requires dedication, patience, and a willingness to confront obstacles head-on. Couples can grow stronger and deepen their commitment to each other by viewing marriage as a ministry that transforms your love from a mere partnership into a sacred calling. By embracing this perspective, you can cultivate a more profound sense of purpose and fulfillment in your relationship, enriching the lives of those around you. As you walk hand in hand with your spouse, you become partners and ministers of love, spreading light and compassion wherever you go. While God wants you to be active in the Body of Christ, the ministry of marriage takes priority, especially during the process of the two of you becoming one flesh.

"For this reason, a man will leave his father and mother and be united to his wife, and the two will become one flesh'? So they are no longer two but one flesh. Therefore, what God has joined together, let no one separate" [1] *(Matthew 19:5-6).*

Couples who interfere with God's will for their marriage find themselves ministering at the expense of their union. Protect your marital borders by working together through a joint effort. Married couples are prime targets on the devil's hit list because of "the power of agreement". Both of you have a target on your back and must unite to shield your home by working together; the devil will use his devices and cunning tactics to dismantle your relationship leaving the two of you in a state of emotional ruin.

God was intentional when he left the back plate off the spiritual armor this is so you can lean on each other to keep your back covered during times of conflict. You and your spouse need to learn how to move in synchronization with heaven. If either of you grants the enemy access, it opens the door for the spirit of sexual perversion to create division between you. Once this happens you will find yourself arguing with your spouse, making statements such as, "I don't feel like you have my back." These words signify the presence of the spirit of division operating in your marriage.

(*Luke 11:17*) *reads "Jesus knew their thoughts and said to them: "Any kingdom divided against itself will be ruined, and a house divided against itself will fall."*[1]

The spirit of division works through vain imagination and distorted thoughts by using God's word against you out of context. If your spouse lacks a servant mindset, they will think too highly of themselves, which in turn will open demonic portals in your marriage, exposing both of you to attacks from the realm of darkness. The spirit of pride will create strife in the marriage, leading both of you to seek comfort in the arms of another person instead of leaning on each other.

WEDDED BLISS!

It is after the honeymoon, and you are ready to settle into building a life with your new spouse. The first couple of months were uneventful. You showered each other with love and affection to the extent that when you were apart, you couldn't wait to be together. This is called the honeymoon phase, also known as total wedded bliss. It is the stage in your marriage where you are so in love with your spouse they can do no wrong. Then, one day, out of nowhere, a big blow-up occurred. The most trivial disagreement brought both of you to your breaking point.

Chapter Six: Sexual Fantasy & Your Marriage

You were willing to stop before things spiral out of control, but your spouse took things to another level by bringing up the past. Their harsh words and insults spoken during the argument left you feeling hurt and heartbroken. This sudden warfare is from the realm of darkness sent to separate both of you, by creating chaos in your marriage. **The way you treat your spouse matters to God**, but remember you are fighting an evil force that can only work in your life if he has a legal right, and when he cannot find a legal right in your bloodline he creates one. In moments of conflict, it is common for emotions to run high triggering the fight or flight response.[6]

One partner may feel compelled to leave the situation, while the other may be ready to fight. This dynamic can lead to tension in the home, followed by the silent treatment once the spouse who left returns. During your time of separation, it is not uncommon for negative thoughts and doubts to take over your mind, creating a cycle of mistrust and anxiety. As minutes turn into hours and hours into days, you find yourselves in separate rooms, while your mind replays the details of your disagreement, reigniting anger and frustration leaving you seeking an escape from these intense emotions.

The turn of events left you feeling as if this is not what you signed up for and as a result of your disappointment. During this time of separation from your spouse. You decide to return to a familiar place in your mind where sexual fantasies still reside. In that moment, you completely forget that God delivered you from the kingdom of sexual perversion. Your Vulnerability takes over, and you allow sexual fantasies in, and before you know it, you are fantasizing about having hot steamy, sex with your Ex, the new employee at the office, a member of your church, a close friend, your favorite movie star, or the neighbor across the street.

Sexual Fantasy & The Christian Mind

Without warning your hands start going where they don't belong but because the sexual imagery of being with someone else is so strong you need to climax. While this is happening your spirit spouse is there cheering you on. This is not the will of God concerning you and your spouse. Instead of arguing to prove who is right or wrong the two of you should have recognized the ungodly patterns developing in your marriage and worked together to address the underlying issues constructively to strengthen your relationship. Both of you should have prayed and rebuked the devil. Although the scripture tells us the married bed is undefiled in (Hebrews 13:46).[1] You are not married to yourself.

What you do with your spouse is honorable in God's sight, but what you do by yourself when you are alone can be seen as cheating. Masturbation is the gateway that leads to a spirit spouse. Please do not confuse this with arousal practices used by a husband or wife to engage in sexual activity with their partner. Sexual acts involving your spouse are not considered self-masturbation. It is your responsibility as a married couple to understand the God-ordained protocol for sex in your marriage it is time for both of you to go before God and inquire of this for yourselves. God wants you to have a healthy sex life because this spills over into other areas of your life, especially ministry.

Take time to deal with the small foxes eating away at the martial vine to avoid getting in a place where you begin rejecting your spouse. The devil cannot make you commit sin, but he can influence you to engage in sin by creating chaos, and situations in your life that pulls you outside the will of God. His job is to destroy the union that God has put together and drag your soul to hell, he is willing to get this done by any means necessary. It is up to you to put on the whole armor of God so that you can withstand the whiles of the devil.

Chapter Six: Sexual Fantasy & Your Marriage

Ephesians 6:10-12 reads,
Finally, my brethren, be strong in the Lord and in the power of His might. Put on the whole armor of God, that you may be able to stand against the [a]wiles of the devil. For we do not wrestle against flesh and blood, but against principalities, against powers, against the rulers of [b]the darkness of this age, against spiritual hosts of wickedness in the heavenly places. [1]

DYADIC FANTASIES

(Matthew 5:27-28) reads, "*Ye have heard that it was said by them of old time, Thou shalt not commit adultery: But I say unto you, That whosoever looketh on a woman to lust after her hath committed adultery with her already in his heart.*" [1]

Dyadic Fantasies cause you to lust after someone else other than your spouse.[3] In the pursuit of wanting to satisfy your partner sexually, you find yourself inquiring about their sexual preferences in the bedroom. Ideally, this conversation should have taken place during your engagement before the wedding. However, perhaps due to discomfort or fear of crossing boundaries, you may have avoided discussing this topic with your fiancé. This may have been done to maintain self-control and resist sexual urges during the dating phase.

Now that you are married, you realize the importance of addressing these differences sooner rather than later. It is becoming apparent that expectations and desires may not align as smoothly as anticipated. It is essential to recognize the significance of open and honest communication about sexual preferences and needs within a marriage to ensure mutual satisfaction and understanding. Dyadic fantasy occurs when two people get married without checking their sexual level of compatibility. One of you may come in at a level one, meaning "Let's just get this over and done with," while the other may come in at a level 10, as in "Choose a safe word."

Sexual Fantasy & The Christian Mind

Being sexually harmonious with your spouse will create symmetry and balance in your marriage. If you and your partner have a different perspective on sex, only one of you will feel satisfied in the marriage, and the other person will suffer from a high degree of sexual frustration. Once this happens, the enemy will then step in and encourage the malcontent spouse to look at porn, which will lead to masturbation, and over time their affection will turn from being with you to self-pleasure, given time this path will lead them in the arms of someone else.

Although you are engaged in spiritual warfare, you still need to communicate with your partner. If you neglect to talk about sex during the dating phase, it is not too late to have that discussion now. Both of you will need to compromise for your sexual needs to be met. The person who is a ten will need to bring it down a few notches, and the other spouse will need to take it up a few notches. This will allow the two of you to meet in the middle.

SEXUAL SATISFACTION

In Africa, couples who are engaged to be married are required to undergo genotype testing to ensure their blood type is compatible with having kids without sickle cell disease.[4] While this testing is not practiced in Western cultures, a new type of compatibility test should be implemented by church leaders, especially when counseling Christians who are engaged to be married. This test should be called the "sexual compatibility test." Lack of intimacy is among the top five reasons couples are divorcing.[5] When two people get married without having an in-depth conversation about their sexual preferences, it can later create big problems within their marriage—leaving both spouses feeling sexually frustrated.

One of you may be a big fan of oral sex, while the other person has never tried it and was told that even in the bonds of marriage, it is an ungodly act that should not be performed.

Chapter Six: Sexual Fantasy & Your Marriage

The same can be said of sexual position, one spouse wants to try every sexual position in the Kamasutra and engage in adventurous sex until they pass out. The other spouse wants to do missionary style to get it over and done with so they can go to sleep. Your sex life feels like a boxing match in one corner you have the traditional, wham-bam-thank-you-ma'am and in the opposing corner, you have the freak of the week. This great divide in sexual preference can leave both of you sexually annoyed with each other. One of you will feel as if your sexual needs are not being met, while the other may feel overwhelmed and insecure because they do not know how to fulfill the other person's sexual desires.

If this continues, both of you will revert to having sexual fantasies about being with someone else who satisfies your needs. After a while, sex with your spouse will feel forced. Over time, this will diminish your attraction to your spouse, potentially leading to increased sexual activity with yourself. Effective communication is the key in overcoming this hurdle. Both of you need to renew your mind and change your thinking. This may not be the sex life you were expecting in a marriage, but all is not lost. One of you imagined your spouse meeting you in the garage wearing only a robe so you can have your way with them against the car or in the back seat.

Then carry them into the house to have more sensual sex on the kitchen table. You desire to have sex with your spouse in every square inch of your home. Your spouse, however, envisioned being married to someone who meets them at the front door, with a hug and a kiss. A person they can enjoy dinner with while talking about office politics, and maybe if both of you get to bed on time you can turn out the lights and have sex for five to ten minutes before going to sleep.

Sexual Fantasy & The Christian Mind

The best way to bridge the sexual gap in your marriage is to share your fantasies with your spouse. When you finally muster the courage to share your sexual fantasy with your spouse, be prepared for their reaction it may be less than enthusiastic. You may hear statements like "You want us to do what? That's gross." Their reaction might leave you feeling rejected, misunderstood, and ashamed. This rejection from your spouse can cause you to retreat into your thoughts, where you will start fantasizing about finding someone more open to fulfilling your sexual escapades.

These fantasies might involve various people, ranging from acquaintances, coworkers, or an old friend from college. The allure of instant gratification from these fantasies will make it increasingly challenging for you to connect sexually with your spouse. Be honest with each other regarding what you need to feel sexually satisfied also, be willing to compromise with the other person by equally agreeing to the new sexual arrangement for your married bed. This will bring an end to sexual fantasies, self-masturbation, and having sex with your spirit spouse instead of your natural spouse.

God wants to be involved in every area of your marriage, take your sex life to him and ask him what is allowed between the two of you, keep the details of your sex life private when and how you have sex should only be discussed with your spouse and no one else. Couples often have difficulties with intimacy because they have invited too many people into their bedroom by sharing intimate details of their sex life with family and friends.

Chapter Six: Sexual Fantasy & Your Marriage

SEXUAL MISCONDUCT IN YOUR MARRIAGE

When the Bible mentions that the "marriage bed is undefiled," it emphasizes the sanctity of sexual intimacy within marriage. This phrase underscores the purity and sacredness of the physical relationship between a husband and wife. It signifies that within the confines of marriage, couples are free to express their love and desire for one another without moral reproach. However, it is crucial to understand that this passage does not imply a carte blanche for sexual behavior in a marriage. Instead, it emphasizes the importance of mutual respect, consent, and fidelity within the marital bond. Bringing another person into the marriage bed does not align with the biblical understanding of marital faithfulness and could undermine the sanctity of the marital covenant.

In essence, married couples are encouraged to cherish and honor their union, recognizing that sexual intimacy, when approached with reverence and commitment, strengthens their bond and empowers them for their shared experiences in life and ministry. The Devil knows God's true intentions for sex within the bonds of marriage and for this reason, he seeks to defile the married bed. The purpose of marriage is to procreate, children born in a Christian home will be raised to serve God which will make them a threat to the devil's kingdom.

He needs a legal right to stop them before they even have a chance to get started and the sexual sins of the parents give him that right. The impact of adultery can create generational curses. Causing all manner of sexual defilement to occur in your bloodline. All sexual misconduct outside of God's will causes the marital walls to crumble which will leave both of you wanting a divorce to escape the weight of it all.

Sexual Fantasy & The Christian Mind

Engaging in any of the following acts can threaten the purity of your marriage.
- **Porn**
- **Masturbation**
- **Adultery**
- **All forms of sexual sins**

Despite the fact you are married these acts are all sinful. Your marriage may work for a while but over time one of you will grow weary of breaking spiritual laws concerning your married bed. Even when it is just the two of you it will always feel like a third person is there. Weird warfare will begin taking place in your home and your children will start acting crazy. Inviting the spirit of sexual perversion into your marriage creates chaos. *"Set your affections on things above and not beneath"*[1] (Colossians 3:2) Do not manipulate your spouse and God's word into being what you want it to be there is a cost for sexual misconduct in marriage.

CRAVING THE TOUCH OF ANOTHER

Sin has a melody that captivates your mind and causes you to operate under a spirit of strong delusion. While the music is playing you feel empowered to dance you feel alive and free it is only when the music stops you realize how foolish you look trying to keep up with its rhythmic vibrations. This is an analogy of sexual sin, it blinds you from seeing the bigger picture. The wife who is led away and enticed by her own lust and whines up cheating on her husband often becomes solely fixated on her lover, neglecting her duties and responsibilities as a spouse. The home begins to suffer as a result of her indiscretion but none of it matters to her. She hates the very sight of her husband and secretly wishes to do him harm.

Chapter Six: Sexual Fantasy & Your Marriage

The more she pulls away from God the more she loses touch with her existence. The more she becomes addicted to her lover's touch the stronger her yearning to be with him increases. She simply cannot get enough of him. He accessed a part of her soul that no other man has ever unlocked, little does she know her lover is an agent of darkness skilled in destroying homes and caging souls. It is as though he holds the key that released her from the prison of sexual frustration. This new lover has awakened all her sexual senses, and she is willing to explore all of them at the expense of her family.

So, she begins lying and stealing time away from God and her family just to fulfill her fleshly desires. She only comes to her senses when she finds herself pregnant or diagnosed with a sexually transmitted disease. This man that she craves so deeply was sent by the devil to destroy her mind, soul, body, and her home by dividing her family. So, what made her step outside the bonds of marriage to seek the touch of another? She was in love with her husband and on fire for God, she walked upright before him and shunned the very appearance of evil.

The devil has no new tricks, the thing that made her commit this sin is sexual fantasies it began in her mind with a thought, and instead of casting down vain imagination, she entertained the thought until one day she was given the opportunity to make her fantasy a reality. The spirit of sexual perversion comes to tear down and destroy especially Christian homes. Now she has to repent to God and ask for reconciliation. She also needs to repent and come clean to her husband by confessing her sins and seek his forgiveness. The same can be said for a cheating husband. Not all men actively seek to have an affair. Sometimes, they are oblivious to the devil's scheme to destroy their homes

Sexual Fantasy & The Christian Mind

A Godly marriage is between two people and unless one of you let a third party in it will remain that way. Oftentimes with men, the cheating begins with playfulness or light flirting. This may take place at work, church, or a favorite restaurant as the flirting increases the husband's attention at home begins to decrease. He becomes less willing to help his wife carry out the daily responsibilities involved in raising a family. This change in behavior at home drives a wedge between him and his spouse as he slowly becomes resentful towards her. Calling his wife a "nag" and other names. He gets upset at the slightest provocation, picking fights so he can grab his car keys and leave the house.

Telling his wife, he needs a break from her and the kids to clear his head. Instead, he wants time alone to meditate on the sexual thoughts in his mind concerning his lust interest that he has been flirting with. Just the thought of her smile, the smell of her perfume, the firmness of her breast, her supple lips leave him fantasizing about being sexually intimate with her. The build-up of his lustful desires leads him to masturbate in his car just to get a release from the intensity of wanting to have sex with this woman. Little did he know the minute he began daydreaming about her. Spiritual boundaries were crossed, and he already committed the act of adultery.

"But I say unto you, That whosoever looketh. on a woman to lust after her hath committed. adultery with her already in his heart."[1]
Matthew 5:27-28

Now that it has already happened in the spirit realm it is only a matter of time before it manifests in the natural and before he knows it. He will find himself in this woman's home or in a hotel room. She will be like hot steam to a congested head. She will feel like a breath of fresh air to him. She will bring all of his fantasies to life with her willingness to do whatever he asks of her. At first, their encounters will feel like total utopia but with time she will demand more by asking him to leave his wife

Chapter Six: Sexual Fantasy & Your Marriage

That is when he will return to his right mind remembering he has a family but unfortunately, this will not be enough to end his double life as a cheater. More than likely he will ghost her and move on to the next. Affairs are like roaches for everyone you see on the counter there are more hiding behind the walls. So, what made this man of God cheat on his wife? Why is he unable to stop the behavior? Why does he do good for a year or two and then fall again? Even after having children outside the marriage. What is preventing him from breaking free of committing adultery? He loves God and his wife, and he wants to please them both. The answer remains the same it all started with sexual fantasies and his failure to cast down vain imaginations, he also succumbed to the sword of defilement in his bloodline.

"Casting down imaginations and every high thing that exalteth itself against the knowledge of God, and bringing into captivity every thought to the obedience of Christ; and having in a readiness to revenge all disobedience, when your obedience is fulfilled"[1]
2 Corinthians 10:5-6

DIVORCING YOUR SPIRIT SPOUSE

At what point did you find yourself ensnared in an unholy union with your spirit spouse? This evil entity is responsible for causing turmoil in your relationships over the years. This demon asserted its hold on you from the moment you engaged in immoral sexual acts. Spirit spouses are tasked with disrupting relationships and destroying households especially those built on faith.[7] These demonic forces become increasingly aggressive in their efforts to maintain control over you, employing any means necessary to divide you and your partner. They aim to ensure you remain bound to them indefinitely, trapping you in a perpetual cycle of sexual sin and moral decay.

Sexual Fantasy & The Christian Mind

You can use the following signs below to check if a spirit spouse is active in your marriage these signs include:[7]

- ➤ **Persistent Marital Issues**: Continual and unexplained marital problems such as frequent arguments, misunderstandings, or conflicts without apparent cause

- ➤ **Strange Behavior or Personality Changes**: Observing unusual behavior or personality changes in one's spouse, such as sudden mood swings, aggression, or uncharacteristic actions.

- ➤ **Recurring Nightmares or Dreams**: Consistently having disturbing dreams or nightmares involving a mysterious or threatening figure that could be interpreted as a spiritual presence interfering with the marital relationship.

- ➤ **Deep hatred towards your spouse**- You find everything about your spouse irritating, even the qualities you once adored during dating. In moments of conflict, you have even entertained thoughts of harming your spouse.

- ➤ **Dealing with Infertility, Bareness, or miscarriage**- The job of a spirit spouse is to frustrate your natural spouse at all cause because they want them gone. As long as you continue to engage in acts of sexual perversion they have a legal right to remain in your life. They do not want to see you procreating with your current spouse. This is the reason you are facing infertility in your marriage although the doctor cannot find anything wrong with either of you.

Chapter Six: Sexual Fantasy & Your Marriage

- **Feelings of Being Controlled or Manipulated**: Sensations of being controlled, manipulated, or influenced by an external force, especially during marital conflicts or decision-making processes.

- **Refusing to have sex with your spouse-** At the start of your marriage you could not resist being physically or close to your spouse, but now you find their presence repulsive. Engaging in sexual activity with them feels like torture and you cannot wait for it to be over so you can pleasure yourself. You often excuse your behavior by telling yourself it is because your spouse is unwilling to carry out certain sexual acts in the marriage. Feeling this way can lead to sexual dysfunction and frequent sexual issues within the marriage.

- **Compulsive Masturbation-** After having sex with your partner, you find it necessary to masturbate, you avoid social events, family gatherings, and going out with your spouse so you can stay home and pleasure yourself.

- **Addition to Porn-** A porn addiction in a marriage can have a negative impact. The use of pornography content can create isolation, and distorted beliefs causing one spouse to neglect the family needs. It can also make sexual arousal difficult during intimacy without the use of porn.

Sexual Fantasy & The Christian Mind

> **Unexplained Financial Hardship-** Once you engage in any form of sexual acts with your spirit spouse. They have the right to blow on your money to create financial hardship for you and your natural spouse, this will feel as if your money is being snatched out of your account from different directions. This is because you committed spiritual adultery, the kingdom of darkness wants you to blame the hardship on your spouse by seeing them as a curse. If you and your spouse fight about money long enough one of you will leave.

> **Intuition or Spiritual Discernment**: Strong intuitive feelings or spiritual discernment indicate a negative spiritual influence within the marriage.

It is important to note that the enemy will lead you to believe these signs are attributed to other factors in the marriage, such as communication issues, stress, mental health conditions, or underlying relationship problems. Therefore, praying and asking God for spiritual insight in revealing this matter to you is crucial. Seek guidance from the Holy Spirit, your spiritual leader, to effectively address any underlying issues in the marriage.

Chapter Six: Sexual Fantasy & Your Marriage

SEX AFTER DIVORCE

The devil aims to keep you in a state of sexual immorality across all aspects of your life until you die. First, he orchestrates intense spiritual warfare against your marriage. Subsequently, his strategy shifts to steering both of you away from each other and towards divorce court. In this battleground, one spouse inevitably invests more time and energy in ending the marriage than they did in keeping the family together. When two people fall out of love with each other, The courtroom becomes the arena where former lovers exert more energy fighting against each other than they do against the enemy.

Upon the finalization of your divorce amiss the emotionally distraught state of each family member, in a strange turn of events you find yourself in bed having sex with your ex, this is a trick of the enemy. How is this possible? You developed a disdain for your spouse towards the end of your marriage and during the divorce proceedings. Now, after your divorce, you find yourself involved in an entanglement. You are now having more sex with them than when you were married. You both said you were tired of each other and wanted out of the marriage.

So, why the sudden change of heart? Once you received your divorce decree in the mail your body started craving your ex-spouse. This is because the sexual soul ties still have you bond to your spouse and the enemy knows this, although you may feel as if you are still married to this person. You are committing fornication. The devil will play with your mind after each sexual encounter the same as he does everyone else. It started with sexual fantasy on a lonely night, once all the commotion ceased with the divorce proceedings.

Sexual Fantasy & The Christian Mind

You start thinking about what it was like coming home to your ex-spouse, and then your mind switches over to the one or two times you had freaky, no-holds-bar sex. The special occasion sex that only occurred during vacations, anniversaries, or birthdays. Snap out of it already, your ex fought harder to divorce you than they did to keep the marriage together. STOP! with the childish behavior of "I love you; I hate you." Committing sexual sin with your ex opens your kids up to demonic attacks that can range from them being addicted to porn to exploring an alternative lifestyle. "Thirty-five to fifty percent of first-time marriages end in divorce, increasing to approximately sixty percent for second marriages and seventy percent for third marriages."[5]

Sex after divorce is a sin. The enemy caused you to divorce each other to stop you from having undefiled sex to being entangled. Now you are on social media updating your relationship status to "it's complicated," God wants you to cut all attachments and walk away but instead, you are choosing to allow the sword of sexual defilement to remain in your bloodline. Having sex with your ex-spouse may feel familiar because they may be the first person with whom you experienced guilt-free intimacy. This is another term for God-ordained sex, it does not necessarily mean the sex was enjoyable, but rather that you felt God's approval and anointing during intimacy with your ex.

Your body melted at their every touch; the tingling sensation of love permeated through your body with each stroke. This was fine and well within the confines of marriage but now that you are divorced the discipline of abstaining from all sexual pleasures is in effect until you remarry.

Chapter Six: Sexual Fantasy & Your Marriage

"For this is the will of God, your sanctification: that you abstain from sexual immorality; that each one of you know how to control his own body in holiness and honor, not in the passion of lust like the Gentiles who do not know God; that no one transgress and wrong his brother in this matter, because the Lord is an avenger in all these things, as we told you beforehand and solemnly warned you. For God has not called us for impurity, but in holiness"[1]
1 Thessalonians 4:3-8.

    Nothing good is going to come out of sleeping with your ex, the minute they move on to a new relationship they are going to drop you like a Tic Tok trend that went out of style. Having sex with your ex gives you false hope and keeps your emotions off balance, the spiritual connection you had is broken between the two of you. It is hard to serve God when you are still lusting and longing for your ex. This dysfunctional pattern of behavior is what keeps a lot of Christians single years after being divorced. Why would God send you a Godly spouse just for you to cheat on them with your ex? STOP! Going back to Egypt because Pharoh wants you back, the next time sexual fantasy hits your mind about your ex, cast it down. God has better for you whenever you are ready to receive it.

Chapter Seven
Overcoming The Guilt & Shame
Eliminating Negative Self-Talk

Your day of reckoning is finally here, and it is time to face the piper. No more running, no more hiding, no more pretending. You have reached your breaking point, and you demand to know the truth. Why do you keep doing this? *"You started running the race with strength, so who bewitched you?"*[1] (Galatians 3:1). Remember the day God saved your soul and put his spirit in you that was the best day of your life. When your eyes finally opened it felt as if you were breathing in air for the first time. Studying his word to become the man or woman of God he called you to be was exciting.

You could not get enough of being in his presence. Now, over the years due to your inability to heal from past childhood trauma, you live life as a mediocre Christian. The Bible reads, *"that we have to be hot or cold we cannot be lukewarm if we are God said he will spit us out of his mouth"* (Revelation 3:15-18).[1] Now you find yourself so far removed from God that committing sexual sin has become your norm. After every encounter, you keep thinking it is the last time. You repent of your sin, thinking you have everything under control until the next time it occurs, and then you realize you don't.

Sexual Fantasy & The Christian Mind

"o wretch man that I am who shall deliver me from this body of death" (Romans 7:24-25)[1]

What is going on and how do you stop? You had no intentions of going this far down the rabbit hole, but it feels like life kept sending you blow after blow and hardship after hardship, trial after trial, and test after test causing you to give in to negative self-talk and sexual thoughts. You gave up on God's promises to establish you.

> *"After you have suffered a little while, the God of all grace, who has called you to his eternal glory in Christ, will himself restore, confirm, strengthen, and establish you"* (1 Peter 5:10).[1]

The pressures of life brought you back to the familiar and without realizing it you return to your old habits of using sex as a coping mechanism to numb yourself from the thorns of life. The trials and tests were only sent your way to prove you and help you mature in God. The day you gave your life to Christ you thought things would change for the better but now it looks like you were wrong to think that. You finally found the missing link in your life the moment God filled you with his presence. When the church leaders welcomed and embraced you this gave you a sense of community, you felt God's love.

So, what happened? Why are you back in bed with the Devil committing sexual sin? When will it truly be the last time? Overcoming guilt, shame, and the negative self-talk that often surrounds sexual fantasies can take your mind on a wild emotional ride. Sometimes, the stuff that pops in your head leaves you feeling guilty and ashamed, it is time to break free from that mental prison and start embracing the freedom to be the person God created you to be. You have work to do, and the Father has need of you in his kingdom.

Chapter Seven: Overcoming The Guilt & Shame

UNDERSTANDING GUILT, AND SHAME

First, let us demystify the trio of trouble: guilt, shame, and negative self-talk. These are like the unwanted party crashers in the realm of our thoughts. Guilt is that nagging feeling that you have done something wrong; shame is the belief that you are inherently flawed, undeserving, or unworthy, and negative self-talk is the continuous loop of criticism playing in your mind.[5] Now, when it comes to sexual fantasies, society has a way of attaching a bunch of stigmas. Maybe it is a religious upbringing, societal expectations, or just plain old taboos. Whatever it is, these factors can lead to a hefty serving of guilt and shame when your thoughts take a detour into the realm of the risqué.

The ministry world is not always known for its openness to human desires. However, fostering an open dialogue within your ministry circles can be a powerful antidote to the shame often associated with sexual fantasies. Create a safe space for honest conversations. It does not mean you have to spill all the juicy details but acknowledge that ministers are humans who fight with the same desires as anyone else. This can be a liberating conversation that will break down the walls of secrecy, and you might find others navigating the same terrain. Mindfulness is not just about meditation retreats and Zen gardens.

It is a practical tool for navigating the daily grind, especially in ministry. Incorporating mindful practices can help you stay present, reduce stress, and gain a better understanding of your thoughts and desires. When sexual fantasies pop up, the very thought should be cast down immediately to prevent these impure thoughts from taking over your mind. Spiritual consciousness allows you to observe your thoughts without getting entangled in a web of guilt or shame. It is about being aware, accepting, and responding according to your Christian values.

Sexual Fantasy & The Christian Mind

SEEKING PROFESSIONAL GUIDANCE

Sometimes, the tangled web of sexual fantasies might require a bit of expert untangling. Seeking guidance from a professional spiritual leader, mentor, counselor, or therapist who understands the unique dynamics of ministry life can be a game-changer. Therapy provides a confidential space to explore your thoughts, navigate any conflicts between your spiritual and sexual self, and develop coping strategies. It is not a sign of weakness but a proactive step towards your spiritual well-being. Embrace your journey, break free from outdated stigmas, and celebrate the complexity of your existence.

Whether you are delivering a sermon, leading a worship band, or daydreaming about your next adventure, remember that you are not alone in the balancing act. A problem shared is a problem solved.[2] Your story is valid, others around you are facing the same struggles. One of the most prevalent challenges individuals face within Christian communities when it comes to sexual fantasies is the experience of guilt and shame. These powerful emotions, often deeply rooted in cultural and religious narratives, can create internal conflicts, and hinder engaging in open and honest conversations about desire.

Guilt, stemming from a perceived violation of moral or religious principles, and shame, which often involves a sense of personal inadequacy or unworthiness, cast a heavy emotional burden on individuals exploring their sexual fantasies within the Christian framework. Understanding the psychological and theological dimensions of guilt and shame is paramount in fostering compassionate responses and creating a safe space for dialogue. Having fantasies is as natural as breathing, it is part of being human. Where fantasizing becomes problematic is when you cross over into the realm of darkness, many of you began fantasizing during your adolescent years.

Chapter Seven: Overcoming The Guilt & Shame

At first, it was calming, soothing, exciting, and fun but now it has taken over your mind causing you to live in a state of sexual immortality. This outlet of escape provided you with a safe mental cave to run into when times get rough. Never in your wildest dream did you think your sexual fantasies would open demonic portals that would create strong holes in your life while giving the devil full access to control you like a puppet on a string.

Here is the cold hard truth you did mess up and you keep messing up, but God does not want you to build a spiritual home on the land of guilt and shame. He wants you to connect to the power source that will sustain you to live a holy life on earth. It is time for you to break free completely by shaking off the guilt, kicking shame to the curb, and silencing your inner critic. Liberate yourself from mental bondage through the power and anointing of the Holy Ghost.

"Likewise, the Spirit helps us in our weakness. For we do not know what to pray for as we ought, but the Spirit himself intercedes for us with groanings too deep for words"
Romans 8:26.[1]

First and foremost, let us establish a baseline truth having sexual fantasies is normal if you are married and thinking about being with your spouse. Anything outside of this will cause you to walk in sexual depravity. Your mind is like a lush maze, sometimes wandering into areas that might surprise you. Your mind is also the battlefield that the enemy uses to wage war against you. Think about it – books, movies, and art are filled with expressions of human sexuality. Your brain is wired to create all sorts of scenarios. This does not mean you are obligated to act on every thought.

Sexual Fantasy & The Christian Mind

Instead of labeling these thoughts as taboo they should be exposed and discussed openly, Sexual Fantasy is a natural part of the human experience but for a born-again believer these fantasies if left unchecked can and will defile your entire being.

"A little leaven leaveneth the whole lump. I have confidence in you through the Lord, that ye will be none otherwise minded: but he that troubleth you shall bear his judgment whosoever he is"
Galatians 5:9-10. [1]

SEPARATING FANTASY FROM REALITY

One key to overcoming guilt and shame about sexual fantasies is understanding the distinction between fantasy, reality, and your Christian responsibilities. Fantasies are a product of imagination, not a blueprint for action. Sexual Fantasies are not from God, it was sent from the pit of hell to torment you by reminding you of what you desire but have no access to at the moment, for those of you who are single this leaves you frustrated until you finally take matters into your hands. Those who are married experience the same level of frustration until they agree to let go of what they have at home to pursue what they think is a better option outside of their marriage.

It is important to recognize these dark thoughts are not yours, these are seeds being planted in your mind to yield a harvest of ungodly behavior. The fruits of these seeds will wreck your life and bring a reproach against the body of Christ. Creating mental boundaries between fantasy and reality will allow you to appreciate and hold to the richness of your Christian values, you will not feel burdened by unnecessary guilt or have to run and hide from your leaders because your imagination is out of control and has taken you on another wild ride.

Chapter Seven: Overcoming The Guilt & Shame

RELIGION AND SOCIETAL EXPECTATIONS

Let us address the elephant in the room – religion and societal expectations. often imposes rigid standards on what is deemed acceptable or taboo when it comes to sexuality. These expectations can contribute significantly to feelings of guilt and shame surrounding sexual fantasies. Guilt and shame thrive in the shadows of secrecy. Open communication with trusted spiritual leaders or friends who are more mature than you will help you to fight and overcome the enemy of your soul, remember there is strength in numbers. Sharing your thoughts and feelings about sexual fantasies will expose the devil and begin your healing journey.

This will foster a mutual understanding and acceptance of your self-awareness and who God intended you to be. If you are married be open and honest with your spouse concerning the thoughts that have been attacking you. Creating a healthy relationship with your partner will give you a safe space where both of you feel comfortable expressing your desires without fear of judgment. This open dialogue will strengthen the emotional connection in your marriage and provide an opportunity to dispel misconceptions and address any concerns that may contribute to ongoing guilt or shame. Knowledge is a powerful antidote to shame.

Often, feelings of guilt and shame stem from misinformation or a lack of understanding about sexuality. Educating yourself about sexual health, wellness, and the diversity of human experiences can be a game-changer. Countless resources are available, from reputable books and articles to educational websites and podcasts. Understanding the vast range of human sexuality, including different preferences and fantasies, can help normalize your own experiences and reduce the negative self-talk that may arise from feeling misunderstood or abnormal.

Take the time to investigate where you are sexual in your life. Have you reached your sexual peak? are you hormonal? Or you are lonely yearning for companionship or just tired of being alone. It is time for you to get in the mirror and face the image looking back at you. Until you are honest with yourself this cycle of backsliding to have sex then repenting and coming back to the fold will not stop. The bigger problem that looms over you is far greater than guilt and shame. It is important to understand that God's mercy is not a toy and should not be played with, you have no idea when it will run out leaving you without a chance to make it back.

Are the momentary pleasures of sexual sin worth your soul burning in hell for all eternity while being tormented by the same demons who lead you there?

CULTIVATING A POSITIVE SEXUAL NARRATIVE

Just as negative self-talk can create a cycle of guilt and shame, consciously cultivating a positive narrative can shift your mindset towards self-acceptance and empowerment. Challenge those internalized judgments and replace them with affirmations that celebrate your spiritual identity in God.

Affirmations include:

- *I am the righteousness of God in Christ Jesus*[1]
  2 Corinthians 5:21

- *I can do all things through Christ who strengths me*[1]
  Philippians 4:11-13

- *the Lord himself, is my strength and my defense*[1]
  Isaiah 12:2

Chapter Seven: Overcoming The Guilt & Shame

In the grand scheme of things, overcoming guilt, shame, and negative self-talk about sexual fantasies boils down to the fundamental truth: accepting yourself as God accepts you giving God your ashes for his beauty (Isaiah 61:3).[1] You gave your life to Christ, yet you still cling to the pain of yesterday; these past traumas continue to affect you by influencing your wrong decision-making. Remember, you are a multifaceted, constantly growing individual, a flawed but beautiful, imperfect human being. Who has been made perfect through the blood of Jesus Christ?

"Christ in you, the hope of glory: whom we proclaim, admonishing every man, and teaching every man in all wisdom; that we may present every man perfect in Christ: whereunto I labor also, striving according to His working which worketh in me mightily."
Colossians 27-29.[1]

It grieves God to see you living in guilt and shame. God wants you to break free from the emotional strongholds that are binding you to sin. He wants you to embrace the natural uniqueness of who he made you to be. Remember that you have the power to end sexual immorality in your life. It is time to liberate yourself from the chains of darkness and societal expectations, whether through open communication, mindfulness practices, or seeking professional support, the path to overcoming guilt and shame is a personal journey of self-discovery and self-acceptance. So, break free, embrace your authenticity, and revel in the joy of being who God has created you to be. You were made in his likeness and his image which gives you the ability to be an overcomer.

"So God created man in his own image, in the image of God he created him; male and female he created them.
Genesis 1:27

Sexual Fantasy & The Christian Mind

LET GO OF THE PAIN!

God sees you and he hears your cry do not confuse a pit stop in life for your destination. Anyone who has ever used the bathroom at a gas station already knows to expect the worst. So, they go in do what they have to do, and leave. Knowing the bathroom at their final destination is a lot nicer. I Corinthians 14:33 reads, *"for God is not the author of confusion."*[1] it comes from the pits of hell. Do not allow the pain and mistakes of yesterday to steal from your promise of a better tomorrow. Your backsliding is no surprise to God he said in his word that he is married to the backslider.

> *"Return, O backsliding children, says the LORD; "for I am married to you. I will take you, one from a city and two from a family, and I will bring you to Zion. And I will give you shepherds according to My heart, who will feed you with knowledge and understanding."*[1]
> Jeremiah 3:14-15

This book is not your personal get out of jail or sin freely all the days of your life card. Sin separates you from God, this is not the plan that he had for you when he placed you in your mother's womb. He wants you to enjoy walking up right before him while on Earth. Psalm 16:11 reads, *"Thou wilt shew me the path of life: in thy presence is fulness of joy, at thy right hand there are pleasures forevermore."*[1] This is what he wants you to have "Joy" forevermore in this life and the one after. This is why he told you to flee youthful lust and pursue righteousness (2 Timothy 2:22).[1] He wants you to live a life of triumph filled with his promise.

Chapter Seven: Overcoming The Guilt & Shame

God could have made sex dull and boring but just like everything else he constructed. He made it enjoyable God wants you to enjoy sex within the bonds of a marriage. He does not want you up late at night masturbating to porn or breaking yourself off with a sex toy because you have been fantasying about your co-worker or someone else all day. God knows the plan he has for you; they are good and not of evil.

For I know the thoughts that I think toward you, saith the LORD, thoughts of peace, and not of evil, to give you an expected end. Then shall ye call upon me, and ye shall go and pray unto me, and I will hearken unto you."[1] Jeremiah 29:11-13

This scripture is the heartbeat of God towards you. He wants to empower you to prosper and give you VIP access to his throne room, but your spiritual garment must be spot-free for you to enter in. The unconditional love God has for you was what held Jesus on the cross, it wasn't the nails. Make up in your mind today to break free from the wiles of the devil. Romans 6:19-20 reads, *"I put this in human terms because you are weak in your natural self. Just as you used to offer the parts of your body in slavery to impurity and to ever-increasing wickedness, so now offer them in slavery to righteousness leading to holiness. When you were slaves to sin, you were free from the control of righteousness."*[1]

Wipe the slate clean and start over, start by praying Psalm 51:1 *"Have mercy on me, O God, according to your unfailing love; according to your great compassion, blot out my transgressions. Wash away all my iniquity and cleanse me from my sin."*[1] Give your Pastor, family member, close friend, or spiritual mentor a call to confess your sins. *"If we confess our sins, he is faithful and just to forgive us our sins and to cleanse us from all unrighteousness"*[1]

Sexual Fantasy & The Christian Mind

1 John 1:8–9. Try not to be shocked if you hear them say "I've been there now let me pray for you." When God forgives you he wants you to walk in the newness of your deliverance. He does not want you wallowing in the memories of your past sins. In Luke 22:31, he told Peter " *Behold, Satan hath desired to have you, that he may sift you as wheat: But I have prayed for you that your faith fail not: and when you are converted, strengthen your brother* "[1]

The biblical meaning of the word desire is to long for, to ask for, to demand.[3] The enemy is asking God for you. He is longing to destroy you, and he even demands that God permits him to do so, but in this scripture, God told Peter, "I already prayed for you." Not only did God know ahead of time you were going to mess up, but he prayed for you so the weight of the sin you committed did not overtake you. As the enemy shoots his fiery darts at your mind, urging you to kill yourself, the father's prayer is sustaining your life. God has so much confidence in you being an overcomer that he encouraged you to share your testimony to help someone else who may be going through the same ordeal and suffering in silence.

God's mercy and his grace kept you. He could have allowed you to die in your sin, but he did not. He still wants to use you in his kingdom. Stop beating yourself up because you messed up. Some of you were born into the spirit of sexual perversion through a bloodline curse. You grew up seeing all the women in your family getting pregnant at a young age. Some of you saw the man in your family producing children and not taking care of them. You had no idea you were operating under a curse of being controlled by spirits from the marine kingdom. You only knew that something did not feel right. But now that you know, ask God to fortify your soul. Do not allow the enemy to lock you in another mental prison of guilt and shame.

Chapter Seven: Overcoming The Guilt & Shame

Romans 8:1 *reads, there is now therefore no condemnation to them which are called in Christ Jesus.*[1]

You have been searching for the answers for years on how to end what you are going through in your body. You knew you were not the one in control of your body because when you did not want to commit sexual sin you would feel something on the inside of you move it felt like a knot in the pit of your stomach. You then heard a voice on the inside of you compelling you to commit the act." Here is the good news God saw you drowning in your sins and rescued you. Get up off your bed of affliction and walk, this is not the end of your story it's the beginning.

The Bible says if a righteous man falls, the Lord will raise him up Proverbs 24:16.[1] You do not have to walk with your head down because God has forgiven you. There is no need to live in fear of the Marine Kingdom because God has already overpowered them. Jesus walked on water, calm the seas. He defeated them more than once and in the end, he will do away with them forever. Revelations 21:1 reads, "Then I saw a new earth, for the first heaven and the first earth has passed away and there was **no longer any sea**."[1] Walk in the liberty of your freedom because God has already given you the victory to do so.

OVERCOMING SEXUAL FANTASIES

During Hurricane season, we stayed tuned to the news watching attentively as the news reporter interviewed victims and their families. Instinctively we are drawn to the rubble in the background. As much as you empathize with the victims your mind cannot fathom the level of mental stamina it will take for them to rebuild their homes. This is where you are right now, your life is in shambles, and although you survived the hurricane of sexual perversion, you are still left wondering.

Sexual Fantasy & The Christian Mind

How long will it take for you to rebuild? Greater works require greater faith. Now that you have a better understanding of what and who you were fighting it is time to elevate your mind so your faith can take you higher. Sexual fantasies are a common and often private aspect of individual sexuality. While these fantasies can be a natural and healthy part of sexual expression within the bonds of a marriage, some individuals may find themselves struggling with unwanted sexual thoughts. In such cases, whether religious or spiritual, your faith plays a significance in helping you to navigate and overcome these challenges.

On one hand, religious teachings can provide a moral framework that guides you in controlling these fantasies. On the other hand, the same teachings may also contribute to guilt, shame, or anxiety when your sexual thoughts or behaviors deviate from prescribed norms.

A Faith-Based Approach

Faith, often associated with biblical application and spiritual beliefs, can significantly influence your attitudes during the rebuilding process. Faith-based teachings guide you toward a healthy mindset in overcoming the sexual sins of the past. One of the initial steps in addressing sexual fantasies within a faith-based structure is cultivating understanding, compassion, and forgiveness. Without this, it is hard for individuals to move forward because of fear of being judged. Church leaders can provide a spiritual perspective rooted in biblical teachings that integrates faith along with prayer and meditation in Psalm 19:14 David's prayer to God was

Chapter Seven: Overcoming The Guilt & Shame

"Let the words of my mouth, and the meditation of my heart, be acceptable in thy sight, O LORD, my strength, and my redeemer."[1]

Meditation calms the mind and clears a path for God to directly speak to you. Incorporating faith into your daily life can be done through your cognitive behavior. This requires you to identify negative thought patterns and behaviors that arise in your emotions. Self-sabotaging behaviors can create problems in your daily life. Allow your faith to serve as a source of strength when reframing your thoughts Align your belief in God to foster a sense of harmony between your faith and your inner struggles. Engaging in fellowship with like-minded believers who share similar values can provide a supportive environment for your spiritual growth.

The sense of solidarity you experience will serve as a powerful motivator for keeping you on track. Faith is a pivotal factor in breaking free and remaining free from sexual fantasies in your mind. You can work towards redefining your sexual values by re-evaluating your moral compass this process involves introspection, prayer, and deep exploration of biblical beliefs. By establishing clear boundaries that align with your faith you can create a spiritual road map for navigating through your sexuality in a way that will lead to spiritual convictions the minute you begin thinking wrong. While faith can provide comfort and guidance, it can also inadvertently contribute to feelings of guilt and shame.

Some religious teachings may emphasize sin or impurity in the context of sexuality, making it challenging for individuals to address their sexual fantasies without experiencing heightened negative emotions.

"Therefore, there is now no condemnation for those who are in Christ Jesus, because through Christ Jesus the law of the Spirit who gives life has set you free from the law of sin and death."[1]

Romans 8:1-2

Self-Compassion

By cultivating a more compassionate attitude towards yourself, you create space for growth and acceptance. Sometimes, breaking free from the clutches of guilt and shame requires expert guidance. Seeking the help of a therapist or counselor who specializes in sexuality can provide a safe and confidential space to explore your feelings without fear of judgment. Therapy offers the opportunity to dive deeper into the root causes of guilt and shame, addressing any underlying issues that may be contributing to your despondency. A trained professional can provide coping strategies, tools for self-reflection, and support tailored to your needs.

The role of faith in overcoming sexual fantasies is a complex and multifaceted topic that requires a mature understanding of both individual experiences and diverse biblical teachings. Ultimately, the integration of faith into the process of overcoming sexual fantasies is a personal embarking that requires self-reflection, open communication, and a willingness to seek support from religious leaders, counselors, and faith-based communities. By fostering an environment of understanding, acceptance, and compassion, you can navigate faith and sexuality in a way that aligns with their values and beliefs, fostering a sense of spiritual well-being and personal growth.

Use the following faith scriptures to bring God in remembrance of his word.[1]

Ephesians 2:8-10
For it is by grace you have been saved, through faith — and this is not from yourselves, it is the gift of God — not by works, so that no one can boast. For we are God's handiwork, created in Christ Jesus to do good works, which God prepared in advance for us to do.[1]

Chapter Seven: Overcoming The Guilt & Shame

Hebrews 11:1-3
Now faith is confidence in what we hope for and assurance about what we do not see. This is what the ancients were commended for. By faith, we understand that the universe was formed at God's command so that what is seen is not made out of what was visible. [1]

Hebrews 10:22-23
let us draw near to God with a sincere heart and with the full assurance that faith brings, having our hearts sprinkled to cleanse us from a guilty conscience and having our bodies washed with pure water. Let us hold unswervingly to the hope we profess, for he who promised is faithful. [1]

Psalm 119:30
I have chosen the way of faithfulness; I have set my heart on your laws. [1]

2 Corinthians 5:7
For we walk by faith, not by sight [1]

Mark 11:22-23
"Have faith in God," Jesus answered. "Truly I tell you, if anyone says to this mountain, 'Go, throw yourself into the sea,' and does not doubt in their heart but believes that what they say will happen, it will be done for them. [1]

Philippians 4:13
I can do all this through him who gives me strength. [1]

Sexual Fantasy & The Christian Mind

Mark 10:27
Jesus looked at them and said, "With man, this is impossible, but not with God; all things are possible with God[1]

Fear is the absence of faith. Believing that you can be set free from all demonic spirits takes work. The Bible tells us that after a spirit has been cast out of a man, he goes to dry places (Matthew 12:43).[1] If you take the necessary steps to get delivered, you will be free. In maintaining your deliverance, you must avoid the things the enemy used to bind you to sin, flee fornication, flee youthful lust (1 Corinthians 6:18).[1] Living a holy, consecrated, set-apart lifestyle is work, but it is possible because the Holy Spirit is the one doing the heavy lifting. It is going to take faith for you to walk this out.

"Now faith is the evidence of things hope for"[1] *(Hebrews 11:1-6).*[1] When God made you he put a grain of mustard seed faith in you (Matthew 17:20-21).[1] Allow God to nurture your faith through his word so you can grow. Ensure you are fulfilling your responsibilities as a Christian believer.

Remember, God's word urges you to *"Wherefore Come ye out from among them, and be ye separate, saith the Lord, And touch no unclean thing; And I will receive you, And will be to you a Father, And ye shall be to me sons and daughters, saith the Lord Almighty.* 2 Corinthians 6:17-18."[1] Take the time to pray for Godly friends, individuals who are destiny fillers, and divine helpers who will assist you in getting to the finish line.

Chapter Seven: Overcoming The Guilt & Shame

FINDING YOUR SAFE PLACE

Now that you have overcome the evil of sexual fantasy in your mind. It is time to find a safe space where you can put down roots and grow. God does not want you to be like a dog returning to your vomit (Proverbs 26:11).[1] He wants you to be a part of his body again so you can join forces with other bible base believers.

Jeremiah 3:15 reads, *"I will give you shepherds after my own heart, who will lead you with knowledge and understanding."*[1]

Open, honest, and compassionate dialogue within Christian communities is essential for fostering understanding, support, and growth. The Christian journey is not meant to be walked alone, and discussions about sexual fantasies should not be relegated to the shadows. The challenges and opportunities for conversations about sexual fantasies within the context of faith communities. Creating spaces for dialogue involves addressing misconceptions, fostering empathy, and embracing diverse perspectives as valuable contributions to a shared journey of faith and sexuality.

From the pulpit to small group discussions, including pastoral counseling sessions to casual conversations between friends, will provide practical guidance for initiating and navigating these essential conversations within the Christian community. Finding your safe space is not easy but it is obtainable. Ideally, this should be the church but if your church body does not believe in deliverance. You can start meeting with a Christian counselor, or you can create a safe space in your home with your family members you can also start a virtual group. Pray and ask the Lord about your next move but remember *"Iron sharpens Iron"*[1] Proverbs 27:17.

Sexual Fantasy & The Christian Mind

Now that you are free it is time for you to share your testimony and let others know that you have overcome by the blood of the lamb (Revelation 12:11).[1] Life has its share of twists and turns, for some of you, the twist hit a little too close to home when dealing with the spirit of sexual perversion. If you have been through the wringer and are looking for a way to catch your breath, becoming a part of the right community of believers is going to be your best option.

There are groups for people who are suffering from drug addiction, alcohol addiction, anger management, and so on. The success rate of these programs is high because participants in the group share similar experiences. They are encouraged to discuss their shortcomings openly without feeling ashamed. The longevity of your deliverance in Christ depends on what you do after you have been delivered. The portal and doors leading to the realm of darkness were closed and sealed with the blood of Jesus Christ during your deliverance. Whether you are in a support group, counseling sessions, or the warmth of a church community.

Rediscovering who you are in God and striving to become that person is going to take work. Philippians 3:14 reads, *"I press toward the mark for the prize of the high calling of God in Christ Jesus."*[1] Overcoming sexual sin is no easy task, on the one hand, you are happy God's grace abounds and gave you a second chance but on the other hand, you want a guarantee that you will never fall like that again. Living a consecrated set apart life can feel like a rollercoaster at times. During your highs, you are confident that you made the right decision to abstain from sex during your years of being single. During your lows life feels overwhelming leaving you filled with the uncertainty of not knowing when or if you will ever get married.

Chapter Seven: Overcoming The Guilt & Shame

If you are married during your moments of triumph when things are going well, you rejoice in knowing you are with the right person but in moments of struggle you find yourself wondering if the sacrifice of being committed to one person for the rest of your life is worth it. Sometimes God will allow you to remain single a little longer than most so you can find out if he can trust you. God already knows whether or not he can, but he wants you to find out. If God called you to a pastoral office and your flesh is not under control. In a matter of years if not months you will find yourself in the middle of a scandal.

God's people are precious in his sight, he does not want you to be a shepherd who violates his sheeps. Some of you will have the opportunity to minister to beautiful women, the kind you see on television or in magazines, some female pastors will minister to handsome men. The kind on reality shows, cinematic movies, and novels. If you are behind the pulpit still dealing with lust, you will act like a horny teenager in high school around these members. The struggles of finding your safe space can be heavy, it can also feel isolating, but if your end goal is to abstain and remain free from all sexual sin then finding your safe haven is worth it.

You are at a pivotal point in your deliverance and with a support group you will be reminded that you are not alone. Being a part of a judgment-free zone will help you navigate the terrains of your deliverance. Despite how long it takes before you get married God is looking at your heart and your desire to please him. This is the reason he delivered you from sexual sin and stripped away the stigma from you and your bloodline. Walk in the freedom and the peace of God that he has given you.

TAKE A LOOK AT THE LIST BELOW TO FIND OUT HOW A SAFE SPACE CAN SERVE AS THE SPRINGBOARD FOR YOU TO MAINTAIN YOUR DELIVERANCE.[4]

- **Spiritual Mentor:** a spiritual accountability partner who is more spiritual and mature than you. Someone you can pray and study God's word with

- **Real Talk in a Safe Circle:**
  Imagine sitting in a room with people who gets it, and are not throwing stones. In these circles, people come together to share experiences, struggles, and victories. No judgment, just real talk.

- **Strength in Shared Stories:**
  There is something powerful about realizing you are not the only one going through this. Support groups offer strength in shared stories. You might hear someone's testimony and think, "Hey, that sounds like me." That connection is a reminder that you are not alone in the struggle.

- **One-on-One Conversations:**
  You may have fallen due to spiritual immaturity, but having access to a spiritual mentor offering one-on-one counseling will help in the future.

Chapter Seven: Overcoming The Guilt & Shame

- **Safe Exploration Zone:**
  Counseling sessions are your safe exploration zones. Dive into the thoughts, explore the tangled emotions, and do it at your own pace. It is a judgment-free space where you are encouraged to confront the issues that have been weighing on you.

- **Finding Forgiveness and Grace:**
  Church communities can be a sanctuary for finding forgiveness and grace. It is a space where the emphasis is on redemption rather than condemnation. Connecting with others who understand the concept of repentance and renewal becomes a crucial part of the healing journey.

- **Spiritual Renewal:**
  For many, healing goes beyond the mind and taps into the spiritual realm. Engaging in prayer, or spiritual practices can provide a sense of peace that transcends the everyday struggles associated with sexual sin.

- **Open Communication is Key:**
  Communication is the secret sauce whether you are in a support group, counseling session, or church community. Be open, share your concerns, and voice your needs. It is like the GPS guiding you on your healing journey.

- **Therapeutic Services:**
  Dive into the world of therapy. Online platforms, community centers, or private therapists offer various options. Find someone who clicks with you – it is like finding the perfect dance partner for the healing tango.

Sexual Fantasy & The Christian Mind

- **Church Programs and Events:**
  Your local church might be hosting events beyond Sunday service. From support groups to counseling services, explore the programs available. It is like a treasure hunt for resources right in your spiritual backyard.

Many of you will read this book and think the notion of finding a safe space is stupid. You may even apply old-fashioned values and say modern-day Christians need to get themselves together and stop playing with sin. The spirit of sexual perversion is affecting the body of Christ as a whole, the level of sexual exposure is overwhelming in today's society. It is time for church leaders to realize this is not their grandmother's gospel. Christian believers are bombarded with more sexual imagery, temptations, and sexual innuendos than ever before. This reality is causing them to engage in sexual sins, many of them are taking trips to the abortion clinic to get rid of unwanted pregnancies. Modern-day Christians possess strong spiritual gifts but exercise little control over their flesh.

"But understand this, that in the last days, there will come times of difficulty. For people will be lovers of self, lovers of money, proud, arrogant, abusive, disobedient to their parents, ungrateful, unholy, heartless, unappeasable, slanderous, without self-control, brutal, not loving good, treacherous, reckless, swollen with conceit, lovers of pleasure rather than lovers of God, having the appearance of godliness, but denying its power. Avoid such people."
2 Timothy 3:1-17.[1]

This generation of Christians believes in drinking when they are out with friends and emulating the sexual acts they see in the media. As much as you hate the thought of knowing they are dealing with the weight of sexual sin. They still need to know that they are not alone and that there is a path to healing.

Chapter Seven: Overcoming The Guilt & Shame

Whether leaning towards a support group, counseling, or finding consolation in a church community, the key is to help them find the right fit, so they do not continue to repeat the behavior and their soul be lost to combat these issues having a spiritual mentor is important for keeping them on the right path. Let these safe spaces become the spiritual womb they need to birth out their ministry, God placed his mark on them to do a work for him in this present world. Someone stood in the gap for you when you were unstable in your spiritual walk with God now that you have overcome the enemy it is time for you to help your brother. I pray the content you have read in this book thus far has blessed you. May God grant you victory over the realm of sexual perversion, empowering you to live according to his spirit.

"I say then: Walk in the Spirit, and you shall not fulfill the lust of the flesh. For the flesh lusts against the Spirit, and the Spirit against the flesh; and these are contrary to one another so that you do not do the things that you wish. But if you are led by the Spirit, you are not under the law. Now the works of the flesh are evident, which are: adultery, fornication, uncleanness, lewdness, idolatry, sorcery, hatred, contentions, jealousies, outbursts of wrath, selfish ambitions, dissensions, heresies, envy,[j] murders, drunkenness, revelries, and the like; of which I tell you beforehand, just as I also told you in time past, that **those who practice such things will not inherit the kingdom of God.**

But the fruit of the Spirit is love, joy, peace, longsuffering, kindness, goodness, faithfulness, gentleness,   self-control. Against such, there is no law. And those who are Christ's have crucified the flesh with its passions and desires. If we live in the Spirit, let us also walk in the Spirit. Let us not become conceited, provoking one another, envying one another." Galatians   5:16-26[1]

Prayer of Repentance

Lord God, you are the ultimate source of praise and adoration. You have crafted me with Your mighty hands and redeemed me through Your precious blood. I confess my transgressions before You as I ask You to forgive me of my rebellious and sinful ways. I have strayed from Your commandments and neglected the truths in Your Word, meant for my guidance and growth in righteousness. I have turned a deaf ear to Your voice and disregarded Your call to live a holy life. I humbly repent of my sin and shame, please forgive me of all my sins. Lord, I am your child, and I ask you to have mercy on me as you cleanse me of my sins. Help me to let go of past mistakes and empower me to walk in alignment with Your will for my life.

I believe that Jesus died on the cross for my sins and that God raised him from the dead. I believe in the baptism of the Holy Ghost with fire is available to all who ask for his indwelling. Cleanse me and wash me from all unrighteousness, renew my mind by giving me the mind of Christ (Philippians 2:5-11),[1] anoint me to live a life that honors you. I am grateful, Lord, for Your unfailing mercies that greet me anew every morning. Despite my unfaithfulness, your faithfulness endures. Purify my heart and fill me with your word, guiding me to walk in righteousness and holiness. Fill me with the precious gift of the Holy Ghost and with fire.

In Jesus' name, I pray,
Amen.

Chapter Seven: Overcoming The Guilt & Shame

PRAYER FOR OVERCOMING CHILDHOOD TRAUMA

Father, in the name of Jesus, I pray right now for deliverance from the hidden pain in my heart, anchored by the impact of childhood trauma. I seek your guidance, strength, and healing touch to overcome these wounds. Please grant me the courage to confront the memories that have stolen my innocence. Please give me the wisdom to understand that my past does not define me. Pour out your anointing on me, O Lord, and wrap me in the warm embrace of your love. May your light shine into the darkest corners of my mind, illuminating the path to healing and restoration. Please grant me the strength to forgive those who have caused me harm and the compassion to understand the struggles that may have led them astray.

Guide me, O Lord, as I navigate the complexities of my emotions. Heavenly Father, please free me from allowing childhood traumas to keep me in a place of stuck causing me to operate out of mental immaturity. End the torment of bad memories that attack me at night, the things that keep me trapped in sexual sin. I rebuke all demonic powers at work in my life and command them to flee from me in the name of Jesus! I declare and decree Isaiah 54:17 over my life: "No weapon that is formed against me shall prosper."[1] Please send your warring angels now to fight on my behalf and free my soul, from any spiritual cage or demonic alters so that I can be free once and for all.

In Jesus' name, I pray.
Amen

Sexual Fantasy & The Christian Mind

PRAYER FOR GENERATIONAL CURSE

Heavenly Father,

In the mighty and matchless name of Jesus Christ, I earnestly pray for the breaking of every generational curse that has afflicted my bloodline. By the omnipotent power of your Holy Spirit, I implore you to sever the chains of bondage and eradicate the sword of defilement from my heritage. Let your purifying fire cleanse my lineage, washing away all traces of iniquity and transgression. Illuminate my path with your divine light, guiding me towards liberation and redemption. Please grant me the fortitude to walk steadfastly in righteousness, shattering the cycle of sin and oppression plaguing my family. I declare and decree that every person in my family who has been affected by the spirit of sexual perversion is free now in the name of Jesus!

God set us free from the prison of secrets that have influenced our actions. Give us the strength we need to tell our story out loud so we can be delivered from the guilt, and shame. Father, I ask right now that as your angels remove this sword from our bloodline protect the younger generation. I break the curse of sexual defilement on my Father & my Mother's side back to the days of Adam and Eve, I forgive my ancestors who committed lewd sexual acts giving the Devil a legal right to defile the members of our family. May your abundant grace overflow within our midst, ushering us into a new era of purity and abundant blessings. In alignment with (Romans 1:4),[1] I receive the spirit of holiness for sexual purity, and in accordance with Romans 6:6–12,[1] I declare my crucifixion with Christ, crucifying all sinful desires of the flesh, lust, fornication, and adultery.

**In Jesus name, I pray,
Amen**

Chapter Seven: Overcoming The Guilt & Shame

PRAYER FOR SINGLES

Lord Jesus,

With a repentant heart, I seek your forgiveness for every sexual sin I have committed. Your promise in 1 John 1:9[1] assures that confession brings forgiveness and cleansing. I ask for your touch to purify my body, soul, and spirit, restoring holiness to my spirit. Thank you for your boundless mercy. I receive your forgiveness gratefully, renouncing Satan's claims over my soul. By the power of the cross (Colossians 2:13–15),[1] I break every chain and stronghold of the enemy from off my life. By faith, I close demonic portals that give the spirit of incubus/succubus accessibility to my life and I cover all entry points under the blood of Jesus. I rebuke loneliness, aloneness, and isolation (during my time of being single) from my life. Heavenly Father, please keep me because I want to be kept until you send me the spouse you have set aside for me. I activate Proverbs 18:22 in my life:" *For he that findeth a wife finds a good thing and shall obtain favor in the sight of God.*"[1]

Father, I am seeking your guidance to abstain from all sexual sin while I wait for my spouse. Help me to resist the spirit of lust, worldly pressures, and temptations. Teach me how to engage in Godly dating to avoid giving into sexual sins, I offer up my body to you, holy and acceptable, I present my body as a living sacrifice to the you (Romans 12:1);[1] help me to trust your provision, timing, and divine plan for my life. Lord, I stand on the reassurance of your promise as I activate Isaiah 60:22 in my life: "The least of you will become a thousand, the smallest a mighty nation. I am the LORD; in its time I will do this swiftly."[1] I declare and decree when it is my turn to marry, things will come together quickly.

In Jesus name, I pray,
Amen.

Sexual Fantasy & The Christian Mind

PRAYER FOR YOUR MARRIAGE

Heavenly Father, In the name of Jesus, I place my marriage in your hands. Thank you for allowing me and my spouse to connect on Earth. I activate 2 Corinthians 1:20 over my marriage: "All the promises of God in you are yes and in you amen."[1] You promise me in your word that my marriage will not be easily broken, so right now, I bind up all the forces of Evil working to destroy my union. I command every spirit spouse to flee out of my home in the name of Jesus. I issue a spiritual injunction right now and command every activity of incubus/succubus to cease in my marriage.

You are not welcome, by the power and anointing of God, I void and veto all legal rights you have to work in my marriage. I frustrated your plans to bring division into my home. In the name of Jesus, I renounce all sexual sins. fornication, masturbation, pornography, perversion, fantasy, and adultery. I break every curse of adultery, perversion, fornication, lust, incest, rape, molestation, illegitimacy, harlotry, and polygamy in Jesus' name. I command all spirits of lust and perversion to depart from all my sexual organs, life, and my home—. I present my body as a living sacrifice to the Lord (Romans 12:1).[1]

My members belong to Christ, not sin (1 Corinthians 6:15).[1]

I activate the refiner fire of God to cleanse all sexual immortality from my life my body and my marriage. By faith, I sever ungodly soul ties with agents of darkness on assignment to destroy my family in Jesus' name. I break all generational curses of adultery from off my bloodline. I take control of my thoughts, binding all fantasies and lustful thinking in Jesus' name. I rebuke and cast out spirits of sexual perversion that aim to break my marital covenant. I close all doors in my life that lead to worldly influence through music, television, social media, and all other platforms used by the devil to plant seeds of lust in my mind.

Chapter Seven: Overcoming The Guilt & Shame

I command the heart of my spouse to turn back to me and away from others, as I turn my heart back to my spouse. God, please remove the scales from our eyes and allow us to see each other in the spirit. Renew our minds concerning our marriage being a ministry and teach us how to minister to each other so that our children and future generations may receive the residual benefits of our love.

In Jesus' name, I pray,
Amen.

Chapter Seven: Overcoming The Guilt & Shame

PRAYER FOR MASTURBATION & SEXUAL PERVERSION

It is crucial not to attempt self-deliverance when dealing with these spirits alone. Their grip runs deep, and trying to expel them alone will likely only displace them temporarily, leaving you vulnerable. Seek the assistance of your spiritual leaders for deliverance from these demonic forces. Trying to liberate yourself from spirits with a stronghold in your life can backfire, worsening your situation. When you cast out these spirits, they will return to inspect in seven days. They will return with even more demons, and if nothing has changed, they have legal grounds to enter, leaving you in a worse state.

During this waiting period, the strong influence within you will resist your efforts to recommit to Christ. Reading the Bible will be hindered by a sudden onset of heavy sleep. Even if you attempt morning worship, disturbances throughout the night will leave you too tired to rise early. Breaking free from these forces will require a collaborative effort between you and a spiritual leader who specializes in deliverance.

"When the unclean spirit is gone out of a man, he walketh through dry places, seeking rest, and findeth none. Then he saith, I will return into my house from whence I came out; and when he is come, he findeth it empty, swept, and garnished. Then goeth he, and taketh with himself seven other spirits more wicked than himself, and they enter in and dwell there: and the last state of that man is worse than the first. Even so, shall it be also unto this wicked generation"[1]
Matthew 12:43-4.

Chapter Eight
The Author's Experience
Where it all began

I was born on the beautiful island of Jamaica. My father was a truck driver, while my mother sold fruits at the local market. I am the youngest of eight siblings, they are all much older than me. So, I grew up alongside their children. Neither of my parents completed high school, but they worked hard to provide for their family. My mother was a Christian to the best of her ability. However, my father was a devilish tyrant who believed in traditional gender roles, where women should be seen and not heard. As a young girl, I idolized him and thought he could do no wrong, but as a woman, I would never want to cross paths with a man like him.

He was a good provider who ruled his household with an iron fist. This made him a terrible partner and father. He had a violent temper that he used to subject my mother to severe physical abuse, nearly killing her on multiple occasions. Unfortunately, during those days, domestic violence was not a priority for local authorities or politicians. One Sunday afternoon, I witnessed a horrifying incident where my father violently attacked his brother with a metal chair during a card game, suspecting him of cheating. The horrific scene was enough to send me running to hide under my bed.

Sexual Fantasy & The Christian Mind

I saw the evil in him that day, though I did not realize I was seeing in the spiritual realm. I was too frightened to tell anyone about what I saw. My Dad had the worst temper with many triggers, anything or anyone could set him off. Perhaps he should have pursued a career in boxing to release his pent-up aggression. In addition to his explosive temper, he was also what one might call a womanizer by today's standards. He pursued the ladies by lining them up like bowling pins, then knocked them down. Leaving a trail of broken hearts in all fourteen perishes on the Island.

He seemed to have no regard for the consequences of his actions, as evidenced by the number of women he impregnated, producing over twenty-plus offspring. I have half siblings all over the Island. As a result of my father's actions, I made a vow never to date or marry a man from the Island of Jamaica, fearing he might be a half-brother from my father's side. My Dad never married my mother, and I believe he had his reasons, although she did not seem to mind because she never loved him. He was a means to an end after her father's untimely death, which left my grandmother destitute.

To secure a better future for us, my mother followed the advice of a stranger she met at the market. Who suggested that she obtain a temporary work visa so she could move to America to escape my father's abuse. The stranger advised her to apply for a work visa and, upon arrival in America, to marry an American citizen to gain permanent residency and then file for us. Leaving the island was difficult for her, knowing she had to leave her children behind to be raised by relatives. However, she felt she had no other choice, as staying would have meant risking her life at the hands of my father.

Chapter Eight: The Author's Experience

ESCAPING ABUSE

After my mother left the island, my siblings and I faced the full force of my father's wrath, now unleashed because my mother finally escaped his abuse. As a child, I could not comprehend the hardships that awaited us. With eight children to care for, our family became too much for any one person to handle. So, we were separated and sent to different homes. My older siblings were sent to live in the city, while my two brothers and I remained in the country. Our aunts, who were mean-spirited and resentful, begrudgingly took us in, but only to receive the monthly stipend my mother paid to our caregiver.

During this time, the exchange rate between the US dollar and the Jamaican dollar made many islanders feel rich when converted to Jamaican currency. My mother sent this monthly allowance to meet our provisional needs until she finalized our immigration paperwork. Eventually, my grandmother grew weary of the constant bickering between my aunts and offered to take us in. I felt a sense of relief, hoping that she would provide the care and support we needed.

My grandmother loved and cared for me because I was the youngest, but she did not feel the same way about my brothers, which deeply saddened me. I could not help but cry whenever she punished them for getting into trouble. She often threatened to send us away because of their behavior. One day, I overheard her telling my aunt that she could only keep us till the end of the summer. This is when the spirit of rejection entered my life, taking root in my heart. I listened as she discussed our departure with my aunt. They decided to separate me from my brothers because my aunt and her husband felt overwhelmed with the idea of caring for all three of us. It was during this time that I began to experience feelings of worry, fear, and anxiety.

Sexual Fantasy & The Christian Mind

I had yet to find out where my brothers would be sent or what would become of them. Questions plagued my mind: Are they going to be okay? Will I ever see them again? Would they have enough to eat? I pondered these thoughts in my heart for days, afraid to ask them out loud.

KEEP IT MOVING!

During this time, I became accustomed to being an introvert. I often found myself being chastised by the adults around me without understanding what I had done to upset them. Even in my silence, the reprimands continued, and it seemed that my presence in their home was an inconvenience. I lived with my aunt for about a year before moving to the city. I was sent to live with my grandaunt the following year. She was my grandmother's sister, but she looked nothing like her. She had a very fair complexion with long flowing hair. From what family members told me, my great-grandfather was an Irishman on my mother's side.

He had fourteen children with my great-grandmother, eight of whom could pass for white, so they married well. This grand Auntie was one of them; she never had children of her own, so she chose the best-looking children from the family to lodge in her home. She was beautiful, and men always flocked to her. She lived in a spacious home with separate maid quarters in an affluent neighborhood. She also owned local businesses, showcasing light-skinned privileges. My first impression of her was that she would treat me kindly. I had no idea she would hate me at first glance because of my dark complexion. I naively assumed that she would treat me well because she was around the same age as my grandmother.

Chapter Eight: The Author's Experience

However, I quickly learned I was mistaken. On the day I moved in, I made the mistake of walking through her front door. She backed me in a corner and told me I should not repeat this behavior. She wasted no time telling me that I was black and ugly and that I should never walk through her front door. She threatened severe punishment if I dared to repeat this action. Initially, I attributed her behavior to her having a bad day, but it soon became apparent that her hatred towards me was unwavering. She reminded me of it daily, despite my mother sending her money for our care.

She ignored our needs and selfishly spent it on herself and others. She allowed my brothers to reside in the back of the home with my male cousins while I shared a room with my cousin near the front of the house. She showed no concern for either of us, using us solely for household chores. While she treated my brothers kindly, I became the focus of her hatred. She controlled the food we received, often rationing portions for us to share. Many mornings, she gave the three of us one boiled egg to share, my brothers ate my portion arguing that I was too slow and did not need it.

MAKE IT STOP!

Over time, I started losing weight, eventually becoming extremely thin. My mother would send me new clothes every three months. However, My grandaunt would give the best items to my cousin, claiming she deserved them because she was beautiful while implying that I was not. This experience marked the beginning of my struggles with low self-esteem. I felt unloved and longed for my mother's presence to shield me from this hurtful treatment.

Sexual Fantasy & The Christian Mind

It was an added layer of anguish on top of everything else I was already going through. As if what I was going through was not enough to make me lose my mind. At the age of nine, I was raped by a family member. He took my virginity and left me scared. It happened late one night, leaving me shaking like a leaf. I was too afraid to tell anyone, so I kept it to myself and prayed asking God to protect me from him so it would never happen again. They hated me, and somehow, I knew if I told them what happened, they would find a way to blame me and tell me it was my fault. I despised my existence and was filled with intense self-hatred, I wished I was dead.

It was during this time the spirit of suicide entered my life. My life lacked the nurturing care of a mother's love. No one expressed affection towards me, nor did they acknowledge my birthdays; instead, each day I survived seemed to bring more punishment. Living in constant hunger left me weak. One desperate day, I resorted to stealing money from my grandaunt's concession stand so I could purchase food at school. I managed to get away with stealing for a while until she set a trap, which I unsuspectingly fell into.

That night she chased me around the house with a belt until I hid under the bed. The merciless beating she gave me left my skin feeling as if it had been set ablaze. I was covered in welts, and the pain made it difficult to walk or sit. At that moment, I wished she had killed me and ended my suffering. Lacking the guidance and emotional support to navigate such cruelty, I developed the characteristic of being a man-pleaser in hopes that it would get her off my back. However, I soon realized that nothing I did would ever appease this tormentor.

Chapter Eight: The Author's Experience

AFRAID OF THE TERROR

Every morning, I crossed a dilapidated bridge on my way to school. As I walked across this bridge, thoughts of jumping off or drowning myself when the water rose after a rainfall, began to haunt me. Living with this woman was driving me to the brink of madness, and I even contemplated running away to escape her cruelty. However, weeks later I discovered that my mother had completed all the necessary paperwork to get us to America. Shortly after the paperwork was approved, she returned to the island to take us to the United States. She managed to get us through customs after which we boarded a plane bound for America.

Things were going great until one day I decided to tell my mom about the hardship I endured on the island in her absence, and without warning, she raised her hand and struck me across the face. She screamed at me, "DON'T YOU EVER REPEAT THOSE DIRTY LIES TO ANYBODY ELSE? YOU HEAR MI!" I was so afraid of the terror I saw in her eyes it looked like flames of fire. That slap drove a wedge between us. Her reaction marked the beginning of a downward spiral and a lifelong struggle where I held a mixture of respect and hatred toward her. She was absent when I needed her the most, leaving me to fend for myself now instead of consoling me, she calls me a liar. What a way to add insult to injury.

This put me in a hurry to grow up so I could protect myself against these abusive adults. The mere sound of her voice became unbearable; despite her religious practices, she attended church on Sundays, praying fervently, but her actions contradicted her faith when she got home. She would yell at me, hurl insults, and call me names. Despite her nightly and morning prayer practices. She still sought help from workers of iniquity. This made no sense in my twelve-year-old brain.

Sexual Fantasy & The Christian Mind

    I lacked the mental capacity to comprehend the situation entirely, but I knew something was wrong. Her marriage to my stepdad only compounded the turmoil. The man she married showed no concern for us and was hostile, he liked pretending as if we did not exist. I did not like him, so I kept my distance. I was mad at myself and the world for not fighting back or speaking up for myself when being mistreated by these grown-ups. I suffered sexual molestation at the hands of different family members multiple times. I felt worthless and useless. I wanted to die, I felt as if the world would be better off without me in it. I looked for ways to make the pain stop.

    I wanted to go numb and not think about any of it. Around this time. I started dating my first boyfriend, who was ten years older than me. I was too young to know that he was playing games with me to get what he wanted so, the abuse continued. He told me he loved me I was not used to hearing this word from anyone. He made me feel special by buying me gifts, and before I knew it, we were sexually involved. The relationship lasted for about a year, and then we went our separate ways. After I broke up with him, I chilled by myself for about a year to recover from my first heartbreak. By the time I reached sixteen, my self-hatred turned into self-rejection and anger.

    During this time, my mom started calling me a slut and treating me like a maid. Every Saturday, I cleaned the house from six in the morning until midnight. This plunged me into feelings of worthlessness, exacerbating my self-hatred. I sought peace by isolating myself in my room with the door shut, the solitude helped me find comfort in reading the Bible. Despite its unfamiliar writing, the words on each page provide me with a sense of companionship. Reading the Bible softened my heart for humanity. I began praying for the strangers I encountered on the buses and trains while on the way to school, God allowed me to see into their lives, so I knew exactly what to pray for.

Chapter Eight: The Author's Experience

One Sunday evening while sitting in my room after attending church. I heard God's voice for the first time he told me I belonged to him, and he wanted to use me. In astonishment, I questioned why God wanted to use a reject like "ME." Out of fear, I told him no; my mom had been strict with me, and I had not experienced life. I asked him to give me three years to live life on my terms, and if he agreed. I will serve him for the rest of my life." God acquiesced to my words and then departed.

TELL NO ONE!

Soon after this experience, I met a guy. He was twenty-six, he was 6'3", with a slim frame, tall dark, and handsome. I was surprised that someone so attractive was interested in me. While I was fond of him, I was not ready to be intimate with him. We did not communicate with cell phones in those days only pagers. He paged me, and when I called him, he begged me to come over to his house. Deep down in the pit of my gut, I heard, "Not to go over there," but I ignored the warning. As soon as I knocked on the door he opened it, grabbed me and pulled me inside, then slammed me against the wall.

He was burning incense while smoking weed. He was taller than me and stronger. At the time, I was 5'6 and weighed 98 lbs. He dragged me to the bedroom, and when I fought back, he slapped me on the right side of my face repeatedly until it burst open; My ear started ringing and it felt numb on that side. He then threw me on the bed, pinned me down with one hand, and began ripping my clothes off with the other. I cried and screamed, but it was to no avail. He had me pinned, and I was helpless. He was too strong, I fought with everything in me, but he still had his way with me. He was drinking a Heineken beer. I hate the taste and smell of alcohol so when he kissed me I bit his lip. My action infuriated him.

Sexual Fantasy & The Christian Mind

He covered my mouth with his hands, and with tears streaming down my face the only thought that came to mind was "Please God make it stop." Finally, it was over. He threw my clothes at me and told me to get dressed and get out. I got dressed at lightning speed. I thought he would unlock the door and let me go, but instead, he backed me into a corner and began making threats. "You better not tell anyone or go to the police." He said, shaking like a leaf, in fear of what he might do next. I nod my head in agreement to keep my mouth shut as if that was not enough to convince him. He added, "I hope you know this is your fault you made me do it." After he released me from the corner. I walked to the front door and stood there in silence.

I was too afraid to speak or look him in the eyes. Finally, I heard the sound. I had been waiting to hear, as the locks opened on his front door. Once he unlocked the door, I took off running until I made it home. By the time I walked through the front door. I rushed to the bathroom and threw up all over the floor. My sister, oblivious to my distress reacted by yelling at me telling me that I better clean up my mess or else. I cleaned up my projectile vomiting, took a shower, and crawled into bed. My body ached from the roughness during the ordeal. It was hard for me to close my eyes the sound of his voice was haunting it left me feeling as if it was happening all over again.

The side of my face hurt because of the open wound from the repeated slaps. My pillow was soaked with tears as I cried myself to sleep. How could I have been so stupid to go to the home of a stranger? A man I just met. I blamed myself for ignoring the inner voice that warned me against going to his house. This guy only lived two blocks over, and I feared running into him again. This fear consumed me for almost a year thankfully our paths never crossed again. I refrained from dating anyone else until my final year of high school when I developed feelings for a longtime friend.

Chapter Eight: The Author's Experience

It was my first experience falling in love, he was different from the rest. Although we started on a good note, after two years we drifted apart. His family disapproved of me and was able to convince him that he deserved better. Once again, I was left feeling rejected, worthless, and unloved.

TIME IS UP!

Shortly after graduating high school, my mother relocated the family from New York to South Carolina. Although I did not want to move, I did not have the financial means to live on my own. Life was calmer in the South compared to the hustle and bustle of Brooklyn. I was now nineteen and had forgotten about my promise to God, but he did not forget. His presence filled the kitchen one night, and he reminded me that his plans for me were still the same and told me that he had work for me to do, and it was time. I tried asking for more time, but my time in sin was up. Although I was involved in teaching Sunday school, reading my Bible, and praying for others, my knowledge of church life was limited.

This changed swiftly when I joined a Holiness church, which unfortunately closed shortly after I became a member due to financial hardship. Despite keeping in touch with the pastor, who lived in Georgia, I felt isolated and lost. Spending my days secluded in my room. I immersed myself in reading the Bible, fasting, and praying. After doing this for three months one day I experienced the overwhelming presence of God. From that day on the Holy Spirit came into my room every morning and taught me his word. He also taught me how to intercede for others. Once I started growing in my Christian walk with God, my family's treatment of me worsened. By this time, I had built a rapport with the church mother who persuaded me to leave my family and move in with her.

Sexual Fantasy & The Christian Mind

She even sent me money to buy a bus ticket. I packed my bag and got on the bus for McCrae, Georgia. Once I arrived and attended a service, I experienced God like never before. I saw the scriptures come alive people were healed and delivered. Witnessing the living manifestation of Scripture, I became convinced of their righteous living. However, my assumptions soon proved me wrong. After spending time around, them outside of church. I realized there was a power struggle between the church mother and the pastor's wife. The pastor's wife displayed characteristics reminiscent of Jezebel. His mother also operated in the same spirit. I had visions and dreams but lacked the understanding to interpret them.

So, I confided in the church mother, believing she was trustworthy. Unaware of her true intentions. I soon learned that she was the primary source of gossip in the church, sharing all the details from one of my visions with her friends, which eventually made its way to the pastor's wife. Once she learned of the visions God had shown me concerning her. She made my life unbearable. In moments of idleness, when the church mother lacked new gossip, she resorted to spreading lies about me. Among the false accusations was the claim that I was attempting to seduce her husband. I had great respect for her husband, I regarded him as a grandfather figure.

Yet, despite my innocence and genuine intentions, her relentless slander tarnished my reputation. As a result, the region became hostile territory for me. Whenever I ventured out to minister and spread the Gospel. People mocked me, branding me as the church slut who was trying to seduce men in the church. She also accused me of wanting her son and her nephew. I could not believe a so-called woman of God was doing this to me. I thought she was a woman after God's heart. So why was she treating me this way? One Sunday, on the way to church, I sat beside a married sister in the van.

Chapter Eight: The Author's Experience

She commanded me to change seats, but there was nowhere else to sit. She got out of her seat, came to the back, and dragged me off the van by my collar. She pushed me through the front door of her house when we got up the steps. I saw the same fire in her eyes that I noticed in my mother's when I was twelve.

PACK YOUR STUFF AND GET OUT!

I found myself in a similar situation, but this time I was older and felt more capable of defending myself. When I reached for the phone to call my mother, she forcefully snatched it from my hand. Grabbing me by the collar, she slammed me against the kitchen cabinets while hurling insults and speaking word curses at me. Once her tirade ended, she ordered me to pack my belongings and get out of her house. I had a hundred and sixty-five dollars to cover my auto insurance bill, but I managed to use it to secure a hotel room for a week. Towards the end of that week, a coworker approached me and told me about a place for rent.

Grateful for the opportunity, I moved into my own space. It was a single-wide trailer with a hole in the floor and no air conditioning. I was determined to make it work despite its shortcomings. The weight of life fell on my shoulders, and I needed an escape so I began fantasizing, after successfully abstaining from sex for over six years. Unexpectedly, I found myself struggling with urges to masturbate. The stress from my situation became overwhelming. I yearned for love and acceptance, which I found by creating an alternate reality in my mind.

Sexual Fantasy & The Christian Mind

I Stopped Going to Church

I refrained from attending church during this time because I wanted to avoid encountering the church's mother. Considering that her son was the pastor, it seemed probable that he would be on her side. Although uncertain, I preferred not to find out. I continued living in the rundown trailer for six months until I was able to upgrade to a better one. However, my excitement was short-lived when I returned home one evening to find a black snake crawling up the wall. The next day, I packed my belongings and left. By then, I had reached my limit. So, I Loaded up my car and returned home. I was in a backslidden state by the time I arrived home and soon returned to my old habits.

Over the next three years, I struggled to recover from the emotional wounds of church hurt. During this healing period, I felt I was disappointing God by not attending church. I believed that I had brought shame to his name by doubting his love for me. Overcome by the mental anguish of feeling separated from God, I decided to reconnect with the household of faith. During this time, I became friends with a pastor who was a true man of God. He had the heart of a pastor. We worked together, and he prayed for me and with me. One day, while praying on the job, the lord spoke to him and told him that I belonged to him and that it was time for me to return.

The Man of My Dreams

I cried when he told me what God said about me, and he then led me through a prayer of repentance. After that, I started attending church again. Eventually, I met someone I thought was my night and shining armor. Little did I know he had the same temperament as my abusive father and for the next fourteen years, I endured his abuse. Despite the hardship, God blessed us with two sons.

Chapter Eight: The Author's Experience

However, after enduring years of domestic violence. He decided to end our marriage by putting me and the kids out of the house to move his mistress and her children in. I was now in my late thirties, going through a divorce, and had to move in with my mother to avoid being homeless. Though hopeless about my situation, I knew I had to remain strong for my children. I vowed not to revert to my old ways of seeking love at any cost. Through divine intervention, things worked out in court, and I was able to afford my own place. Two years later, God blessed me and the kids with a home. It was during this time I came across the book "Destroying the Spirit of Rejection" by John Eckhardt, which helped me heal from childhood trauma.

I was finally getting delivered from the pain of my past. For the first time in my life, I was in a good place. I should have been happy, but something in me would not allow it. It was December and I sent the kids with their dad for the Christmas Holiday. Out of nowhere, I was overcome with loneliness and aloneness. Tears streamed down my face as I sat on the sofa at home alone. Wondering why I was single again. What was wrong with me? Why could I not find love? It had been years since my divorce, and no one had shown any interest in wanting to date me. Maybe my ex-husband was right—when he told me I would spend the rest of my life alone because I was "black and ugly, and no man would want me."

I was very unhappy with the outcome of my life. I felt like a failure, who was disappointing everyone around me, including God and my kids. Instead of silencing the negative thoughts, I allow them to consume me. A few days later, I reluctantly decided to try online dating. Soon after creating my profile, I connected with someone. He told me he had been divorced going on four years and would like the opportunity to get to know me.

Sexual Fantasy & The Christian Mind

I enjoyed conversing with him, it provided a welcome distraction from my stressful life as a single parent. He was a deacon at his church who sang on the choir, this seemed promising. He appeared to be a good catch—friendly, calm, and easy to get along with. Our initial dates went smoothly until he embraced me, and I felt myself giving in despite my initial reservations. I had abstained from sexual intimacy since my divorce, and I did not want to compromise myself or disappoint God. Nonetheless, we continued talking regularly. He was very supportive of my commitments and interests, which impressed me.

He was very cunning because he was on assignment for the devil while professing to be a man of God. I let my guard down and let him in. As he showed more kindness, my feelings for him grew. His generosity caused me to fantasize about being with him sexually, and you know what they say: Wherever the mind goes, the body follows.

I FELL

My body fell right into his arms. There are two main reasons why I strayed from God and fell into the enemy's trap. While there may be other contributing factors, these are the primary ones. First, I let myself become exhausted from doing ministerial work, which weakened my spiritual defenses. I constantly engaged in prayer, assisting others, and counseling. After tending to the needs of the people, my focus shifted to nurturing my children, aiming to raise them as God-fearing Christians, and law-abiding citizens. The second reason was that I allowed people to use me until I was completely depleted.

They took advantage of me until I had nothing left to give. Their constant demands left me feeling lifeless and empty. I had no energy left to fight or resist the devil. There was no room for me to express my vulnerability. I was expected to be a pillar of strength at all times.

Chapter Eight: The Author's Experience

It felt as though I was a large body of water, and everyone around me came with the biggest containers they could find to make withdrawals. When I reached my breaking point, they dismissed my feelings by saying, "You're stronger than this," "You're a powerful woman of God; you shouldn't feel this way," or "Look at how God uses you." I desperately needed to have a meltdown moment without being judged, but unfortunately, that was not possible. I was not allowed to break down I had to be the personification of strength and resilience everyone expected me to be. So, when the enemy started sending crazy thoughts to my mind, I found myself too weak to resist.

I felt pressured to give them the version of Rica they wanted to see—a persona that appeared to have everything together and under control. Being transparent or showing raw emotions was not allowed. I learned the hard way you can't heal what you conceal. Despite knowing this, I allowed negative thoughts to linger, and before I realized it, I found myself "drawn away and enticed by my own lust (James 1:14-15)."[1] Unknowingly, I was backsliding I grew tired of being who God called me to be. It was overwhelming, and I was growing weary of being single. This is why I remained in an abusive marriage for fourteen years.

It was out of fear at the prospect of being a single mother. I despised my singleness, it felt like a curse. I just wanted to fall into the arms of a partner to feel loved and supported by having him put his arms around me while whispering in my ears. "Babe, I got you! Take off the cape you don't have to be superwoman today." I felt like a prisoner of isolation and loneliness, so I made up my mind that day. I was done being the tower of strength everyone wanted me to be. I was done being their prophet on demand. It was clear they did not care about me because they made more withdrawals than deposits. Even when I felt the walls of life closing in on me and could not breathe when the warfare was warfaring, when I felt like I was about to lose my mind.

No one cared! No one picked me up in the spirit. They kept telling me how blessed I was because I was a single mom who owned a home and drove a nice car. I woke up one day and decided I did not want to be her anymore. I did not want to be "Prophetess McPherson." I hate her, the cost of being her was too high, the praying, fasting, worship, and spiritual discipline proved to be too much. Caring for God's people when it felt like no one cared for me in return was too much, and I was tired. I needed to be with someone who did not know me, someone who would allow me to be anyone else but her. She was suffocating me, and I needed a break.

The moment I decided to commit sexual sin, I backslid in my mind first, then my body followed. A true man or woman of God can not commit sexual sins while still connected to the Holy Spirit: "Know ye not that your bodies are the temple of the Holy Ghost (1 Corinthians 6:19)." My fall began with each thought I entertained without casting down. Once I began acting on these thoughts, the spirit of God departed. Leaving me with a gift but no anointing until I repented of my sins and returned to the body of Christ.

THE BETRAYAL

The decon I met on the dating app charm worked, and before I knew it, I felt like giving him full access to the core of my being. The Bible tells us that our gifts are without repentance (Romans 11:29). After our interaction, I started feeling that he was married because he began behaving differently. He could only talk during the daytime, ignoring calls at night and on weekends. He stopped answering his calls at night by responding with an "I am busy and cannot talk right now text."

Sexual Fantasy & The Christian Mind

When I texted him on a Friday, he would respond on Monday. His behavior no longer aligned with that of a single man. He only prioritized spending time with me when he wanted us to spend the weekend together. This confused me, causing me to believe his lies. It seemed implausible that a married man could disappear for three days without his wife noticing or objecting. I struggled to discern the truth, haunted by the memories of my ex-husband's infidelity. I did not want to inflict this level of pain on another woman by being with her husband. Despite my suspicions, he convinced me I was imagining things. Tired of being alone and longing for companionship, especially when my children were with their Dad.

I reluctantly accepted his version of the truth. I liked having someone to spend time with however, I could not shake the feeling that he was married. So, I prayed, asking God to reveal the truth. Shortly after praying, he sent me a receipt for a reserved room, providing me with his full name and other details. Armed with this information, I searched online until I found the truth. I was devastated to discover that I had fallen into the arms of a married man. My worst fears were confirmed as I gathered the evidence I knew with certainty that I had fallen into the enemy's trap. My worst fears came to pass, and I was now an adulterer.

I was shocked to realize I had been involved with someone else's husband. My heart raced with disbelief. How could I have fallen so far from grace? Confronting him with the evidence I found online, he responded without hesitation, revealing his true narcissistic nature. He dismissed my concerns, claiming the information was incorrect and insisting that he had been divorced for four years, blaming the internet for not updating his status. I was deeply hurt by his lack of remorse. Instead of apologizing, he shifted the blame to me, accusing me of not trusting him and invading his privacy by investigating his past. Feeling betrayed and devastated, I blocked his number.

Sexual Fantasy & The Christian Mind

After this, I remained in bed for three days wondering. Why was this my portion? why was sex my drug of choice? and how could I rid myself of it once and for all? How could I have thrown away all those years of celibacy? Refusing to leave my bed until I figured out the answers to these questions. God began speaking, revealing the sexual patterns in my family's history. He told me no one talks about it, but this has been in my bloodline for generations. He showed me the connection to the marine kingdom due to my origins of being born on an island. Additionally, he revealed that I was spiritually bound to a "spirit husband," preventing me from appearing as single and available in the natural realm. Moreover, God unveiled a memory from my teenage years, of me sitting in a social studies class, daydreaming about sex.

This marked the beginning of my relationship with sexual fantasies, serving as a coping mechanism whenever I dealt with fear and insecurity. This revelation shed light on my struggles and provided clarification on how to break free from destructive sexual patterns. God also showed me how I did not protect my gates with what I watched on television and the conversation I engaged in at work: "Evil communication corrupts good manners"[1] 1 Corinthians 15:33-34. After this ordeal, I went into counseling, hoping to get help in putting it all behind me as I rebuilt my life quietly. One day, while cleaning up the house, in an open vision God showed me the title and cover for this book.

I quickly dismissed it, but I kept having the same vision over and over again. Then I heard God say, "I want you to write a book titled **"Sexual Fantasy and the Christian Mind**. "I immediately started pleading with God "Please do not do this to me I have learned. my lesson, I promised never to do it again." pleading with God to let me put it quietly behind me and move on with my life. You have called me to walk in the prophetic office, people will make a mockery of me." In the middle of my pleading, God allowed me to feel the weight of his glory and he said to me.

Chapter Eight: The Author's Experience

"Rica, this is not about you it is about my people who are suffering in silence with sexual sins because they are ashamed. Many of them are stuck in a cycle of going back even when they don't want to." I want you to share this information so they can break free." As God was speaking to me he began showing me Christian believers sitting in their rooms crying asking for help and pleading for answers, he also showed me believers with titles attached to their names aborting babes out of fear of being exposed. They were afraid of the shame attached to being pregnant while single and saved.

I knew then that I had to put my feelings aside and do what God was asking me to do, I knew that I would be judged and criticized for writing a book on a subject that so many consider taboo. The church may even have a barbecue, cookout, and a bond fire in my honor, but I know the voice of the God I serve, and I am here to do his will and no one else's. I fell prey to the sins of sexual perversion that were set in motion before my existence on earth, surviving a tumultuous childhood filled with hurt, pain, shame, and disappointment only made matters worse. Today, I can boldly say that I am delivered and set free from sexual sin, I desire to please God and live holy for the rest of my days until he call me home.

NOTES:

NOTES

Introduction
What to Expect

1. "Ephesians 2:8-9 (ESV)." *Bible Gateway*, www.biblegateway.com/passage/?search=Ephesians%202%3A8-9&version=ESV.

2. "Psalm 51:5-10 (KJV)." *Bible Gateway*, www.biblegateway.com/passage/?search=Psalm%2051%3A5-10&version=KJV

Chapter 1
Understanding Sexual Fantasy

1. *BibleGateway.com: A Searchable Online Bible in Over 150 Versions and 50 Languages.*
www.biblegateway.com

2. Chery, F., & Chery, F. (2023). 80 Epic Bible Verses About Lust (Flesh, Eyes, Thoughts, Sin). *Bible Reasons | Bible Verses About Various Topics.* https://biblereasons.com/bible-verses-about-lust

3. *Sexual Fantasy | Encyclopedia.com.* www.encyclopedia.com/social-sciences/encyclopedias almanacs-transcripts and-maps/sexual fantasy#:~:text=A%20sexual%20fantasy%20is%20an,are%20fully%20conscious%20and %20recognized.

4. Wamsley, Erin J. "How the brain constructs dreams." *eLife* vol. 9 e58874. 8 Jun. 2020, doi:10.7554/eLife.58874
https://www.ncbi.nlm.nih.gov/pmc/articles/PMC7279884/

5. Grover, Sandeep, et al. "Unusual cases of succubus: A cultural phenomenon manifesting as part of psychopathology." *Industrial psychiatry journal* vol. 27,1 (2018): 147-150. doi:10.4103/ipj.ipj_71_17

NOTES

https://www.ncbi.nlm.nih.gov/pmc/articles/PMC6198602/

6. Admin. "Proverbs 30:28." *Let God Be True!*, letgodbetrue.com/proverbs/index/chapter-30/proverbs-30-28. https://letgodbetrue.com/proverbs/index/chapter-30/proverbs-30-28/

7. "Flee - Definition, Meaning and Synonyms." *Vocabulary.com*, www.vocabulary.com/dictionary/flee#:~:text=We%20get%20the%20word%20flee,the%20scene%20of%20the%20crime

8. "Dictionary.com | Meanings and Definitions of English Words." *Dictionary.com*, 18 Oct. 2021, www.dictionary.com/browse/reprobate

Chapter 2
The purpose of sexual Fantasies (The Erotic Mind)

1. *BibleGateway.com: A Searchable Online Bible in Over 150 Versions and 50 Languages.*
www.biblegateway.com

2. Foy, Terri Savelle. "Sexual Soul Ties." *Cfaith*, www.cfaith.com/index.php/blog/25-articles/relationships/18095-sexual-soul-ties

3. "Exotic — Definition, Examples, Related Words and More at Wordnik." *Wordnik.com*, www.wordnik.com/words/exotic

4. "What Does Mark 6:18 Mean? | BibleRef.com." *BibleRef.com*, www.bibleref.com/Mark/6/Mark-6-18.html

5. Blender, Bible. "Under Pressure From Herodias, King Herod Takes the Head of John the Baptist (Matthew 14:1 - 14:12) - Bible." *Bible Blender*, 30 Aug. 2023, www.bibleblender.com/2019/bible-stories/new-testament/matthew/king-herod-takes-the-head-of-john-the-baptist-matthew-14-1-14-12

NOTES

6. *Mind Control Spirits - FREEDOM From Mental Attacks on the Mind.* www.demonfreetoday.com/mind_control_spirits__freedom_from_mental_attacks_on_the_mind

Chapter 3
Childhood & sexually

1. *BibleGateway.com: A Searchable Online Bible in Over 150 Versions and 50 Languages.*
www.biblegateway.com

2. "Census.gov." *Census.gov*, 20 Feb. 2024, www.census.gov

Chapter 4
Masturbation: The power of a touch

1. *BibleGateway.com: A Searchable Online Bible in Over 150 Versions and 50 Languages.*
www.biblegateway.com

2. Michael. "Marine Spirit." 10 Jul. 2010, https://undarkblog.files.wordpress.com/2014/03/marine_web.pdf

3. Deep Believer. "MIND CONTROL Is Real! Millions Are Being Mind-Controlled by the Marine Spirit." *YouTube*, 13 Aug. 2022, www.youtube.com/watch?v=_hBwa_Ao1EM.

4. Professional, Cleveland Clinic Medical. "Masturbation." *Cleveland Clinic*, my.clevelandclinic.org/health/articles/24332-masturbation
https://my.clevelandclinic.org/health/articles/24332-masturbation

5. *15 Signs That You Are Under the Attack of a Spirit Husband and Wife - Family - Nigeria.* www.nairaland.com/4321675/15-signs-under-attack-spirit

NOTES

6. Grover, Sandeep et al. "Unusual cases of succubus: A cultural phenomenon manifesting as part of psychopathology." *Industrial psychiatry journal* vol. 27,1 (2018): 147-150. doi:10.4103/ipj.ipj_71_17
https://www.ncbi.nlm.nih.gov/pmc/articles/PMC6198602/

7. *Primary Steps to Demonic Possession.*
www.johnhamelministries.org/Primary_Steps_Demonic_Possession.htm

8. Choosing Therapy. "Soul Ties: Types, Signs, & How to Break Them." *Choosing Therapy*, 9 Jan. 2024, www.choosingtherapy.com/soul-ties

Chapter 5
Godly Dating

1. *BibleGateway.com: A Searchable Online Bible in Over 150 Versions and 50 Languages.*
www.biblegateway.com

2. "How Sex Drive Changes Through the Years." *WebMD*,

3. "What Ages Are Women and Men at Their Sexual Peak?" *MedicineNet*, 14 Dec. 2021,
www.medicinenet.com/what_ages_are_women_and_men_at_their_sexual_peak/article.htm.

Chapter 6
The Effects of Sexual Fantasies on Your Marriage

1. *BibleGateway.com: A Searchable Online Bible in Over 150 Versions and 50 Languages.*
www.biblegateway.com

2. "---." *Dictionary.com*, 16 Dec. 2020, www.dictionary.com/browse/vow.

3. Mark, Kristen P. "Extradyadic Relations." *Springer eBooks*, 2014, pp. 2102–05.

NOTES

https://doi.org/10.1007/978-94-007-0753-5_972

4. Munung, Nchangwi Syntia, et al. "Perceptions and Preferences for Genetic Testing for Sickle Cell Disease or Trait: A Qualitative Study in Cameroon, Ghana and Tanzania." *European Journal of Human Genetics*, Feb. 2024, https://doi.org/10.1038/s41431-024-01553-7

5. *Hello Divorce | Online Divorce Without Expensive Divorce Lawyers.* hellodivorce.com
6. Center, Maria Droste Counseling. "Relationships and the Urge of 'Fight or Flight'" *Maria Droste Counseling Center*, 1 Feb. 2021, mariadroste.org/relationships/relationships-fight-or-flight-urge
7. *Deliverance From Spirit Wives and Spirit Husbands (Incubus and Succubus) | Upper Room Fire Prayer Ministry.* www.upperroomfireprayer.org/prayers/spirit-wives.

8. Jackie Redd. "Sample Wedding Ceremony." 29 Jan. 2007. https://www.flgov.com/wp-content/uploads/notary/sample_ceremony_eng.pdf

NOTES

Chapter 7
Overcoming the Guilt and Shame

1. *BibleGateway.com: A Searchable Online Bible in Over 150 Versions and 50 Languages.*
www.biblegateway.com

2. *Joanne Harris Quote: "A Problem Shared Is a Problem Solved."* quotefancy.com/quote/2007566/Joanne-Harris-A-problem-shared-is-a-problem-solved#:~:text=Joanne%20Harris%20Quote%3A%20%E2%80%9CA%20problem,shared%20is%20a%20problem%20solved.%E2%80%9D

3. "---." *Dictionary.com*, 17 Sept. 2020,
www.dictionary.com/browse/desire

4. Diocese, Newcastle. "Creating a Safe Space: A Christian Perspective to Managing Anxiety - Newcastle Diocese." *Newcastle Diocese*, www.newcastle.anglican.org/creating-safe-space-christian-perspective-managing-anxiety.php

5. BetterHelp Editorial Team. *Understanding Potential Root Causes and Effects of a Guilt Complex | BetterHelp.* 2 Mar. 2024, www.betterhelp.com/advice/behavior/what-is-a-guilt-complex-and-5-signs-you-have-one.

Chapter 8
The Author's Experience

1. *BibleGateway.com: A Searchable Online Bible in Over 150 Versions and 50 Languages.*
www.biblegateway.com

Made in the USA
Middletown, DE
23 June 2024